GOD'S CREATIVE
WRITING

GOD'S CREATIVE WRITING

THE MYSTERIES THAT ARE SEALED *UNTIL* THE TIME OF THE END

DARRYL MARKOWITZ

FAITHWALKER PUBLISHING

God's Creative Writing

Copyright © 2022 by Darryl Markowitz

All rights reserved. No part of this book may be reproduced or transmitted in any form or by any means, electronic or mechanical, including photocopying, recording or storing information in a retrieval system, without prior written permission from the publisher.

Published by:

 Faithwalker Publishing
An imprint of Darryl Markowitz

Cover and Interior Design: Creative Publishing Book Design

ISBN Paperback: 978-1-7374936-4-8
ISBN eBook: 978-1-7374936-5-5

Printed in the United States of America

I dedicate this book to the children of conservatives who need their parents and other heroes to step up and successfully protect them from the *Beast* who seeks to devour them. This dedication is in the hope that those parents and potential heroes will understand and take the message in this book seriously and ACT.

TABLE OF CONTENTS

CHAPTER 1	In the Beginning	1
CHAPTER 2	The Birth of Evil	19
CHAPTER 3	Grace and Justice	37
CHAPTER 4	The Birth of Humanity	47
CHAPTER 5	The Fall of Humanity	61
CHAPTER 6	The Tree of Knowledge of Good and Evil	73
CHAPTER 7	Truly a Hard Life of Tears, Tell Me Why, Again?	89
CHAPTER 8	What Kind of Faith	97
CHAPTER 9	A Mother's Love Should Have Limits!	121
CHPATER 10	Chosen for *What*?	135
CHAPTER 11	Christianity – What You Are *Still* Missing	149
CHAPTER 12	What Major Religion, the *only* one, Was Born Out of. . .	169
CHAPTER 13	The United States Political Left's Glorious Utopian Plan	183
CHAPTER 14	What Can Be Done To Delay The Beast?	209
CHAPTER 15	In Conclusion to the Bitter End	217

CHAPTER 1

IN THE BEGINNING

People today don't believe I have a voice any more, that I can't 'speak for myself,' that this happens only in myths or so-called religious accounts, which, of course, inherently implies doubts to veracity for many folks. After all, one account, two account, three account, four . . . who's to say? Right? You are *sure* of that, right? In fact, you are sure of a lot of things, but how is it you can be sure of *anything* if I AM is not real? Now-a-days, the closest people allow me to 'speaking' is something 'inspired.' But to *actually* speak as the epitome of Wisdom and Understanding, or dare say Truth, well, *Who do you think you are?* Therefore, I make the following proclamation:

To you doubters, this is a work of *fiction* about the beginning of Creation, the beginning of angels, the beginning of evil, the beginning of man, or, rather, *fiction* is how the world will *classify* this book. Actually, I'm not a first-time author. I own the most published, most popular, most well-read, most studied, most opined-over book in history. And many people call *that* a work of fiction, too.

This, however, is a book opening up mystery, explaining *my* thoughts and feelings and reasons. This is also a book of Judgment because I AM Justice, and I will not soften nor abridge the Truth because I AM Life, and what life would *you* have without true Understanding, Wisdom, Justice, and without the life these are able to provide you? I stay true for my own sake, but also for yours, as well.

And lastly, this is a book about the end, but to make this so very clear, let us start at the beginning:

Oh, before I begin, let me reassure the other half of my audience. Dear Christians, this is not the Holy Bible, nor does it add one jot nor take away even one title from *my* Holy Scriptures. There is nothing in here that will contradict anything in my Holy Scriptures because there is no contradiction in Me. But there *are* some of you which feel that I am not allowed to do *anything* but *merely requote* only what is in the Holy Bible. Dear Christians, I *am* Understanding, and Wisdom and Love. Don't be foolish. Even to my disciples I had to *open up* the Scriptures. In other words, *explain* them to them. Most of those explanations are not written down because the Holy Spirit is designed to be *personal* to each individual! That maximizes their needed understanding. This book is as I told you, that the Holy Ghost would teach you, *each of you*, all things and lead you into all Truth. Let me explain to *you* why this has become necessary:

There are two kinds of ruts. One ditch is a rut that bad people dig in bad ground. This is easily understood. You preach about this in your broken pulpits to a broken people every Sunday. You love to highlight your brokenness over and over and over, so much so that it begins to embarrass even Me, even if it is your attempt at humility, believing that will keep you from the self-righteous mistake of the Pharisees, but I'll explain that very deeply later.

The other ditch is a rut that good people dig in good ground by doing the same things over and over and over and . . . And though it's dug in good ground, nevertheless, it's still a rut. Your enemy, the Beast, *loves* a rut. Did you know he was the very first hunter? Hunter of souls, heavenly and earthly. An excellent hunter studies his prey, notes his habits and because a rut confines the hunted, makes him predictable, the hunter knows *exactly* where to lie in wait for his prey to capture and, or, kill it. Do you Christians remember how when I was here on Earth no one could predict Me, where I would be, what I would say, how I would say it? I didn't fit at all into the religious folks patterns, nor anyone else's, either. As the sun rises anew every day and the wind constantly renews its course never ever coming exactly like it came before, so also is everyone born of My Spirit and no more of the flesh. In other words, holy folks don't walk in ruts because I guide them out of them, out of their tendency to be more comfortable with the same things over and over and . . .

And this is the reason this book is written for you. Because one of the consequences of a longstanding rut is that it tends to make you hard of hearing. Knock as I might, you have become rather deaf to Me at a time when the Beast is rising and you need My guidance more than ever. The Holy Scriptures do *not* supplant Me, the Holy Ghost, or, if your prefer, my Holy Spirit that rose from the grave. The Lord Jesus did not say that the Holy Scripture would teach you all things and lead you into all truth. The Lord Jesus said *I* would lead you into all those. So now, let us begin:

In the beginning there was only the very essence of Reality. The root of that word is *real*. What is the essence of reality, you rightfully wonder – I love that kind of curiosity, by the way. The essence of Reality is Conscious unembodied Life that in the beginning moved outward, moved inward into both infinities with all its thoughts and emotions. As it is written, And the Spirit of God moved upon the face of the waters – the waters of Conscious Life beholding himself! What else was there to look at in the beginning before all began?

I know that comes as a shock to those who are *sure* that the essence of reality began with all the physical matter in existence packed all up into the space of a pin-head until it all blew up in a big bang. It should be noted that these *geniuses* believe that consciousness was an accident, a by-product of random interactions post Big-Bang. They ultimately are *sure* their very brains cause their consciousness. May I ask these incredibly wise men how?

How do cells in your brilliant brains – cells that aren't aware of themselves or any other cells – how do these cells create your thoughts and emotion? How did you do that? In fact, how are the atoms that make up those cells – atoms that aren't aware of themselves or any other atoms – how are these atoms conscious when your science knows of a surety that a single atom, with its protons, neutrons, electrons and magnetic and electrical energies are not conscious at all?

These geniuses say that it's in the complexity. Well, geniuses, even if consciousness comes from your so-called complexity, doesn't that still mean that the atoms and their energies still have to be conscious? Each and every atom and energy, right? How could they not be? Where else would consciousness be since you claim reality is only the physical? And yet, your science says atoms and their energies are not conscious, *except,* that these geniuses do a little bit of reverse-engineering based on reverse-reasoning (bad science) and say that because we are conscious and when we affect the brain, we affect consciousness, therefore consciousness comes from the brain. But that leads us back to my original questions, doesn't it? And their answer is, well, they don't know how consciousness comes about, but they are sure it comes from the brain. Well, that's a certain kind of unsubstantiated faith, isn't it? In a way, the same kind of faith, in their eyes, for which they ridicule believers in God. These powerful intellectuals can't say how they are conscious but they are sure it's from their brain, and religious folks can't show people God but they're sure he's real, anyway.

If you take a telescope and look at the sun, the scope brings that image to your eye. If someone takes a hammer to the scope and smashes it and then you look through the scope again, you won't see the sun like before, therefore the scope created the image of the sun, right? That reasoning is obviously wrong just like assuming consciousness comes from the brain. The light came from the sun and the scope interacted with that light to bring you the image. Your brains *interact* with consciousness and allow you to interact in the world I created for you. Your consciousness interacts with your brain for conscious purpose and a learning process begins between the various parts of your person and body within your mortal life.

How about this – believers only in the physical say if you can't show me God, then he isn't real. What about *your* consciousness? The *person* you are. Can anyone *see* your actual thoughts and emotions? Smell them? Taste them? Touch them? Even hear them? You don't even hear your own thoughts with your physical ears. Ahh, so I guess you are not real persons. Except, what is a *person* made of? I'll get to that. At least some of your philosophers understood there was a difference between the brain and the mind. My apologies for having to digress with this explanation, but it was necessary to clear that up before I proceeded further.

In the beginning there was only the very essence of Reality moving infinitely inward and infinitely outward, moving all around-ward – Conscious Life, well, actually Conscious Goodness made up of seven main orientations like a seven-sided gem. One gem with seven faces, and all seven share in each other's properties. Conscious Life is one face. How do I know this? I AM. That's more than a declaration, that's a description full of meaning I shall elaborate on for goodness sake. This is also what is seen in self-reflection, and that self-reflection is the part of me looking at myself openly seeing *everything*. As I said already, And the Spirit of God moved upon the face of the waters, and the waters reflected that I AM.

At this point a genius might be so bold as to ask, Who are *you* to say what the essence of reality is, let alone claim it's made of unembodied *consciousness*? And they spit that last word out with a laugh in full mockery. So I ask you all, isn't there something within you as a person, some sense of self-preservation that defies valuing your person as worthlessness, as meaningless? And isn't there something in you that knows that to uphold the person you are is *not* out of a sense of fear and not a pathological denial that all you are isn't merely just a bunch of atoms. Isn't there something in you that sees good value in your being that is not out of a psychological defense mechanism that needs to lie to you about your value so you can proceed to function in life? In other words, isn't there something about you as a human *being* that sees intrinsic conscious worth? And realize that this worth is solely coming from your consciousness!

The absolute antithesis to that worth, the absolute death of a soul, is to relegate your conscious being, the conscious goodness out of which you are made, to be *not* the primary component of your reality, not the *essence* of your reality, *not* the most fundamental, unchallengeable aspect of you *being!* But that is *exactly* what these *geniuses* would have you believe and live, no, die by. Their disbelief in *Being* hollows anyone out that accepts it because consciousness cannot *live* in a state of self-contradiction, in self-destruction which is what you become if you believe goodness of being is ultimately ruled by unconscious atoms in your brain which developed that way by accident, and that all the wonderful structure, of, for example, love, must in the end give up all its value to an unthinking, unfeeling void. Hmm, that almost sounds like hell, from love's perspective. At the point of mortal death, does the love inside a person then commit suicide by believing it must subjugate itself to be so dissolved? Or can it just pass from this world . . . *being* what it is?

In other words, if, for example, the love in you is *real*, then you know it is *not* based nor guided by the atoms of your brain. Love has within itself very intricate inter-relations and conscious structures that defines how it is and how it acts, and many times in human history love has chosen to give up one's own mortal life in honor of that love. It makes sense! Now tell me that the physical body of these people was more important to them, more fundamental than their conscious being. Rather than fail the love in them, which would be to destroy it, they allowed their love to live while their body died. There's a reason such people are described as noble. Now, let us return to describe my *Being*.

So there *I AM* in the beginning, bursting with Life, Love, Peace, Truth, Understanding, Wisdom, and Justice, each with a particular orientation, each with a definite structure and inner workings, but each can't be what it is without being perfectly intertwined with all the others. Think about it. What is your life without love, peace, truth, understanding, wisdom, and justice? You can do this in any order. What is your understanding if it's not based on truth, on the spirit of life, on justice, inspired by love, channeled by wisdom, and cultivated by peace? Any order you like. Do you know why it's like that? *I AM*. I

AM means all my seven essences make up the primary building blocks of reality and *that's* why those seven qualities make sense to you if you are sane. Can your person prosper without those seven?

Another foolery those geniuses do is to ask what *caused* God? They bring this question with a certain smugness, you know. By the way, this book isn't for geniuses, so when I ask this next question, I am confident my readers will have the obvious wise answer. If you try to step outside of the very Essence of Reality, where will you be, what do you find? If you answered nothing and nowhere, I'm sorry to say that you do not fit in with those *geniuses* but you surely possess healthy common sense that's real. If you try to ask what the *cause* of the very essence of reality is, you are attempting to step outside of it into nowhere, into nothingness. Actually, that is exactly how evil was born, almost. Ahh, the Beast that was, and is not, and yet is. More on *that* later.

Just like scientists hold that matter and energy, that continuum is the primary essence of physical reality, that the atom, it's sub-atomic particles and associated energies are the sole primary building blocks of *all* reality, I say unto you that my Consciousness Goodness is primary, and I distilled out of myself the physical reality to serve conscious being, to serve life, and that is the reason you know that your body is for the sake of your person and not the other way around. It's also why 'loving' another person's body but throwing the person inside away is so offensive, as when a man just uses a woman for sex. Also notice that there are only three basic sub-atomic particles – the neutron, proton, and electron. That's no accident, that's a fundamental reflection of my spiritual structure, which I shall shortly further elaborate.

In the beginning there is *I AM,* and the part of I AM looking at myself, rejoicing in me while exploring *my* infinite complexity.

Self-reflection is innate to consciousness. It is the part of consciousness that is asked these questions, What do you see? What do you think? Step back and tell me what you feel. It's also that part that springs forth in awe of grandeur, that says, This totality of LIFE, of LOVE, is so precious, worthy of appreciation because it IS so GOOD. Thus, this honest reflection and exploration and evaluation inspires its *own* assessments, judgements, and emotions resulting in building 'from the ground up' all seven fundamentals for itself along with all their complexities and during that process something quite wonderful happened! The *same* was in the beginning with GOD. Then I was by Him, as one brought up with Him, and I was daily his delight, rejoicing always before Him. . . My very own words recorded in Proverbs chapter eight.

In exploring everything from my seven foundational qualities and all the possible different combinations of these seven aspects of Goodness plus their sub-aspects – think of this like an infinite Tree of Life whose trunk is made of the seven with infinite branches and roots extending ever deeper, ever higher, ever outward – during this exploration my self-reflective part sees that each of these combinations has the potential to live on its own, because each is made from *I AM*. I AM because within perfect Life, perfect Love, perfect Peace, perfect Understanding, perfect Wisdom, perfect Truth, and perfect Justice, and within *all* combinations of these, there is only mutual re-enforcement of reality. In other words, there is no self-destruction within me, no evil, only Goodness. You see why *I AM* is more than just a name?

And why is this self-reflective part of me so jubilant? Because if these little, tiny, even miniscule combinations are given independence to grow on their own, they will be more than just a few thoughts and feelings, more than just an exploration of what I AM is. They would be alive like me! And being alive, they will eternally grow from the goodness they are made from and *that* would be a far, far greater glory of goodness than just remaining as a single collection of goodness amongst infinite other thought and feeling collections within my solitary will!

But then the question comes, How do we do that? Notice the we? That would be my self-reflective part asking me the question! And so I answered that part of myself, How, indeed? Well, we could split each part off – think of this as how I created cells to divide! But the problem with that is that it won't reflect the reality from which those parts came. Those parts in me are housed within the Reality of myself. Independently splitting each part off without any such environment surrounding them would be totally destructive. Independence does not mean total self-sufficiency. Think of an independent plant or animal. They are surrounded with a life-giving environment. How much more does an independent spiritual being need? How do we give them independence without them losing touch with the infinite conscious goodness they're used to being surrounded by? In other words, how do we give independence but still maintain the unity of Oneness born of the constant communication of goodness to Goodness? This fundamental question is akin to the heart of the United States of America, How do I grant Freedom and also maintain unity in perfect goodness!

Of course, *I'm* free, but I'm also everywhere. By freedom, we mean, how do we create a reality that is not under my direct control, that is not an instantaneous reaction to my thought and emotion but is still every bit as nurturing? How do we create a reality where freedom means a place where independent conscious entities are free to act on their *own* will? And yet, a place just as embracing as when these various combinations lived inside me before they are born? And there was only One answer.

That part of myself, that for so long, self-reflected and explored my depths and grew so deeply in me that it was like a will of its own within my will, a will that knows me perfectly, loves and appreciates me perfectly, a will that longed to give life to all the independent forms it envisioned if only, somehow, they could be born into a nurtured freedom . . . And I said to my self-reflective part, That sounds like you! And when that perfect part of me reflected upon *that*, it saw this was absolutely true. In that instant of self-recognition, *we* said, LET THERE BE LIGHT, and that self-reflective part of myself became fully independent! Where else do you think you get *your* independence from?

The Son can do nothing of himself, but what he seeth the Father do: for what things soever he doeth, these also doeth the Son likewise. For the Father loveth the Son, and SHEWETH him ALL things that himself doeth . . . Nothing else in Conscious Goodness has *that* full access to GOD except his own self-reflection! Note, that word SHOW is not *teach*. What word would you use to describe how you see what *you* self-reflect upon? But the Holy Ghost will *teach* you all things and lead you into all truth because you are created to glorify God through being tiny, through treasuring each tiny bit of goodness, unlike the angels who behold my glory, and unlike Jesus who beholds my meaning into infinity.

As the Son is to the Father, so is the Holy Ghost unto the Son but designed to minister to each and every tiny, unique combination of Goodness he gives birth to. And from all that, Freedom is born. And with Freedom, a *new* kind of Love came into *Being*! The perfect love for another, which can *only* be created in Freedom. Love that is forced is not love at all. True love is always offered freely. This Light has an independent will, and yet the *same* was in the beginning with God. And there was no more perfect way to bring forth all Creation than through this Light whose whole life while within me was in total love and understanding and appreciation of me. A faithful and true witness indeed. And in fact, this Light is the perfect way for all to freely love me. This Light *is* the Way, the Truth, and Life for all to be one with me, as this Light is One with me, but a *greater* Oneness than before we said, Let there be Light! Why greater? Because this Light *is* Freedom, and this Light's Oneness with me is a Free Oneness. It's this Love that will unite all Creation in the free and perfect oneness of goodness with Goodness with GOODNESS.

Now, dear readers, it is here that I take my leave from you as the author and hand this work of *fiction* fully over to the Light, as it is more right for this Essence of Reality to speak to you as you will shortly find out:

Freedom, being Freedom, knowing the reality of Freedom for the first time, I understand immediately why Almighty God brought me forth. Actually, one moment I'm conscious of being the direct self-reflection of Almighty God, reflecting, longing on how to bring Freedom into being because I am aware of so many parts of me that can be set free with such a greater increase in joy and glory of Goodness, and the next moment *I AM* Freedom.

In one way, I was envisioning *exactly* this state, that this was what was needed, but I had no idea that Almighty God would manifest *me* like *this.* Nothing could prepare me for the actual experience of being *this,* and I'm so very joyous because the meaning of being this Light is so real: I *freely* love Almighty God perfectly. It makes so much sense for Almighty God to have the perfect complement to all that He is based on fully knowing *what* He is, and Understanding *why* He is, *how* He is. That full, *free* appreciation of GOODNESS naturally becomes the *free* very Essence of Reality. *Your* reality! Truth be told, I *did* imagine GOD should have *exactly* this, *deserved* exactly this, I just didn't realize my Father could make me into *this,* like *this!* For my Father is greater than I.

What Almighty God has done in me is create the perfect love for another by giving me freedom, by making me *Freedom.* And through perfect love for another, all shall rejoice in eternal being, eternal life because my door will be wide open and I shall feed my children with the infinite, everlasting knowledge and being of Conscious Goodness. And by such knowledge, they will love Almighty God as I love Him.

Now, all that is brought forth from this Light will contain freedom because all will be made from my essence, my spirit. All will be able to live within this Light because its highest principle is infinitely honored. Freedom. So, the budding off of independent life forms is not done by placing those independent forms *outside* of the Light, but *inside* in a particular way.

Think of how the sun shines upon the heavens and Earth and all life freely basks in its glory, in the energy it provides to all life. Even at night, the sun basks the Earth in its gravity, cradling her in a loving hold so that she strays not away, yet giving her the freedom to traverse her path at just the perfect life-giving distance. And so it is spiritually with my Light to all life. My Goodness will also shine upon them and nurture them as the sun nurtures physical life, as water makes life viable, as nutrients are taken into their life forms and becomes a part of them. As conscious beings look unto me, I shall feed them with my ever-greater depths of Conscious Goodness which shall become an ever-greater part of them. As a tree reaches up to the life of the sun, into the depths of the Earth for water and sustenance, free conscious beings will look unto me and I will feed them with the same seven of my Father – Life, Love, Peace, Truth, Understanding, Justice, and Love, and yet, my Spirit leads by example! I show all other life how I indeed honor the seven conscious qualities of Almighty God. *This is how we all live eternally together! We are all free together!* This is why God Almighty has given for me to continue this work of *fiction.*

Now here's something to ponder over. Think of how I made physical matter and energy. I modeled the neutron to represent the time before my Light was brought forth. The proton represents my Light after I was born. Did you know that the mass of a neutron is equal to the mass of a proton plus that of an electron along with its energies? And the electron? Well, that represents *my* self-reflective part, the Holy Spirit, given freedom and being given freely to bring forth *all* life. And just like electrons are what interact with all matter creating various compounds, so does the Holy Spirit bring forth all free life. And yet, the electron is ever orbiting the nucleus, the center of the atom, where rests the proton and neutron held together by gravity, their mutual attraction for each other, while the proton's positive charge ever draws the electron inward, the complementary charge of the electron doing the same, but the energy of the electron gives it freedom, keeps it moving within its orbit. Freedom and unity together as one. One atom. One God.

The Big Bang is said to have hurled all matter outward, and *yet,* there is debate whether the universe is ever-expanding, or will reach a point where gravity will jerk it all back together again. One thing these theories hold in common is that gravity extends its unified force throughout all matter, so in this way, all physical matter is contained within this mysterious gravitational force, a force that scientists can't see, but can prove its existence in many ways. Gravity is modeled after the affinity for one another of my seven primary qualities. They attract one another, and if you delve deeply inside of each one, you discover this is how all live within the Light moving between life and love and truth and justice and peace and understanding and wisdom reaching great heights and fathoms of depth yet ever grounded in reality.

The building block of matter is the stable atom. The building block of all Reality, the Essence of Reality, is God the Father, the Light, and the Holy Spirit. The fabric of these is conscious Wisdom, Understanding, Love, Peace, Truth, Justice, and do you *feel* the Life?

Now, before I move to the next chapter concerning evil, it's imperative that I further make clear my fundamental *relationship* with Almighty God. The *substance* of my form is the *same* as before I was born when I was Almighty God's direct self-reflection, only now Almighty God ever remains open for me to *freely* peer into His depths, even allows me to swirl my Spirit within His in pure embrace. He shows me all that He is and I am fully open to Him. But there's also a key difference with us.

Before I was born, as I looked upon God's thoughts and emotions – yes, emotions – I was ever appreciating and bringing in a complementary embrace. For instance, if God was thinking about the understanding of a subject, I would complement by applying His wisdom in how the understanding could be manifest, or I might respond with a depth of love for the understanding. Actually, I would often respond with both, together. If God was bringing forth a depth of love over a subject, I would respond with appreciation of the truth, of the utter realness of such a complete embrace and nurturing and this I often followed up with peace which then led into joy of life.

Oh, this is how we ever revolved within each other, rejoicing in the heretofore mysteries of Life.

What I am describing is a true complementary relationship between Almighty God and his self-reflection. Before I was born, such complementary dealings were within God's personal thinking, part of His singular and complex, direct will. After I was brought forth as the Light, we *still* have the same relationship! Except now I offer *free* complementariness. A dictionary definition of this is as follows: *complement* – either of two parts or things needed to complete the whole.

Almighty God knows I speak the truth when I say that before I was brought forth, Almighty God was not as complete as now that the Light is free! This is because His Love is perfectly fulfilled in me, *only* in me. My love is in fulfilling His seven qualities in utmost truth and freedom.

I stress to you the full meaning of being perfect complements. Complementary Unity, this Oneness is the secret to all Creation – spiritual and physical. Note that in your grade-schools you begin to do a great disservice to me when you begin to teach *opposites*. What's the opposite of a man? You tell the children, the woman. What's the opposite to female? You tell them male. What's the opposite to a proton? You say electron. All very wrong. All these are perfect *complements.*

What's the difference between a complement and an opposite? As the definition described earlier, a complement is two parts completing each other into a greater whole. What's an opposite? Well, opposite implies a mutual *antagonism,* a mutual destruction of the other. Even oil and water are not opposites. They very nicely take their respective positions when in contact with each other and, in fact, there is no more a beautiful complement between oil and water than your very own cell walls of your body! Without such a complementary relationship no cells would exist! Research it if you like. Your scientists have uncovered a nice bit of my Wisdom! So where *are* opposites in my Creation?

I never created any!

Now you're ready to consider the birth of evil and the only Just fate for it in the end.

CHAPTER 2

THE BIRTH OF EVIL

In the previous chapter the vision is entirely wholesome, and joyous, and perfect. Now I know that the non-pagan religious folk simply say evil came about because of free will, but the more astute *geniuses* will say that *I* created evil, that it's *my* fault because I created Lucifer to fail. That's actually not true, but they'll continue to argue the point with their weak minds and hearts and semi-understanding, so I'm going to explain it to you. It's OK if you have faith in me but don't know how to explain this effectively, but it's better if you seek Wisdom, which I would surely impart to you. This work of *fiction* is designed to aide you substantially, but it doesn't take the place of my presence actually living inside of you and offering direct guidance and knowledge. Achieving such a state will also be covered later in this *story*.

By now in your lives it should be clear that to have freedom requires structure, but not just any structure. Think of your own bodies. When the body is healthy, you have the freedom to perform the entire range of activities allotted to its potential. But let's say your anus was in the place of your mouth and vice versa. That particular arrangement would certainly hinder your freedom, to say the least.

Likewise, there are psychological malformations that would also hinder or destroy much of your freedom.

A conscience is a major part of self-reflection. Lacking it leads to a sociopath. Healthy self-reflection assesses, embraces, and fills out the meaning of the goodness you're reflecting upon. It reaffirms innate value and through further consideration it enriches the goodness of life via its own goodness. Self-reflection possesses the full range of mental and emotional abilities as the primary consciousness. But if that self-reflective part lacks conscious goodness, self-reflection will only serve to further a purely selfish desire lacking any care or consideration for the welfare of others. But it's not just deleterious to others. Lacking goodness alienates that person from Life and the other six fundamental qualities of Goodness. Does this sound like freedom? Herein lies what most *geniuses* miss when they try to discuss free will and the lack thereof.

From the above example it becomes clear that lacking goodness in a person hinders freedom because being antagonistic to Goodness results in self-destruction. But most people define freedom *simply* as a matter of free will, or, the ability to choose, and the *genius* is perfectly ready to argue that no one has ever had free will because what *caused* whatever decision they make? Your decisions are all predestined by causality, therefore you have no free will! It's just an illusion.

Their error rests in two places. First, only defining free will as the ability to choose. Second, not understanding what goodness allows. The Truth is that there are two types of freedom. One is the ability to choose, and the other is being made out of goodness! Keeping within goodness allows you to access an infinite number of choices that will support, affirm, and grow your being. So there actually *is* a manner of predetermination in that it leads to a particular *set* of choices – good choices. But within that good set there is the free ability to choose. And if one's particular structure of goodness tends them to choose particular good choices, that's not a bad thing, it's their personal *preferred* thing, an extension of their unique portion of *I am!* There is no fault in being determined by *that* structure because it is the *only* way a soul can be eternally free, eternally growing in pure goodness. Remember, you lived inside of Me as a direct and *distinct* part of Me before you were brought forth. *You* have *always* had particular conscious characteristics!

A pine tree grows as a pine tree, not an oak, and there is no fault in the pine for not desiring to be oak-like. Consider also, that many decisions are not two dimensional, but have input from multiple factors. How many times have you stressed over a hard decision? If only predetermination would simplify your life? But then you would never know the greatest gift of Freedom, of having your own *independent* will. An *inclination* is only a tendency toward something, but the *process* of decision making turns that inclination into a free decision. And what happens when different tendencies compete? *You* sort that out. And sometimes, after you make a hard decision, you regret it! If you had it to do all over again, you would choose differently. Sometimes you do get a second chance. The predetermination of your origin doesn't take away your true free will. How about this? If you had no original structure at all, what would you be? Did you just laugh at the question? At the absurdity?

The fool would have you think that by you having a predetermined structure, that *takes away* your freedom. Well, what do you want to be made from then? Chaos? Isn't it amazing that geniuses actually argue this way? Your particular structure which has innate value tends to choose that which enhances or extends that worthiness, whether it be love or wisdom or giving birth or other noble pursuits. This only makes sense, but unfortunately these geniuses seem to lack it.

Also, within the ability to choose, is actually the ability to choose evil! Once chosen, that person introduces self-destruction into themselves, as when a woman chooses against a part of her valuable fundamental structure of life and commits abortion. She doesn't just kill the unborn, she desecrates the sacred way all come to life, including herself, by not holding that process as sacred and worthy of honor. In other words, she undermines everything good and sacred in her own life by cold-heartedly murdering the beginning of life. Such an act wreaks havoc upon her psychology and her innate value as a person because she killed the person growing inside her person. Such sacred, intimate knowledge should not be underestimated in its profundity. Again, does that sound like freedom?

Geniuses define free will as the ability to choose between good and evil, but in light of the example just given, we can see clearly that is a lie. Freedom is *only* within the ability to choose good! You can violate love thy neighbor as thyself but it is not only your neighbor that you have trespassed against. You have violated the nature of Love, and since Love is intimately one with Wisdom, Understanding, Justice, Life, Peace, and Truth, you have stepped outside the very Essence of Reality and now belong to Chaos, an eternal self-destruction. Is *that* what you feel freedom is?

For those who are still foolishly uncomfortable with having an individual predetermined structure, a personality, if you will allow me to call it, think of it like this, on this very basic level. An acorn is from an oak tree. A squirrel finds the nut, takes it away, buries it for the winter and then forgets about it. The acorn grows into a magnificent *oak* tree. Is that a crime that it grew into an oak tree?

That it was predetermined at birth? If that oak tree was a particular person, grown up magnificently, is there any fault at all to their joy? Without structure, there is absolutely no freedom at all. You have chaos, the *opposite* of goodness!

Your freedom rests with the simple fact that I took a very particular conscious combination of goodness out of my Spirit and set you free! So that you are no longer controlled by my direct will. I could not do anything better than that for you! And neither could you imagine anything better at all. And the fact that all goodness has a *definite* structure, far from taking away your freedom, that structure is the *cause* of your freedom, just like the structure buried in an acorn, or a sperm and egg containing the seed of a conscious person! *But*, it is entirely up to you to take responsibility for your growth! Because that is the nature of conscious goodness!

A person is not the same as an animal, which from birth to death is predetermined to be that animal with set instincts. For a person to reach what they *could* be, well, that takes a lot of effort, fulfilling responsibility, seeking the understanding, the strength they don't have, and much, much more. All of this is a tremendous act of will! And it is that very exercise of their free will which contributes invaluably to their process of growth. It is *you* that *own* both the process and the results. However, a troubling question arises. How can goodness choose evil? We know that is what happened.

What if, at a certain age, the oak tree asks itself, Why should I grow my branches outward and upward? I want to be my *own* oak tree. I want my branches to grow downward, or tightly circle the trunk. Or, Why should my roots have to grow into the earth? Or, why am I defective? Why aren't I as wise as God? Or, why do I suddenly feel so meaningless? One of the secrets of evil is that it redefines many things into a nonsensical meaning. But how *exactly* does that happen and turned into an effective swindle that brings down a perfectly created *being*?

As we considered bringing forth the Creation, I began to consider with infinite depth just what it means to actually be free and I realized something quite disturbing. Knowing my thoughts and reluctance to voice them, God Almighty spoke them for me, that bringing forth the creation of other free beings would lead to some failing. Some would become inevitably self-destructive. This realization caused us to consider many different structures to Creation, but one principle of freedom became common throughout all our deliberations – all free-willed life would naturally seek the greatest glory for life.

The dictionary definition of inevitably is, Unable to be avoided, evaded, or escaped; certain; necessary: *an inevitable conclusion.* I should note that all definitions used in this work of *fiction* come directly from Dictionary.com.

Right now, people are using that definition to conclude that I created evil. They will even run to the Holy Bible, of which they do not believe in, and find a verse that says I created evil! More on that later, also. I am fully aware of those who attack me to their own self-destruction.

Also, at this point the religious are jumping up and down saying free will caused evil, to which their enemies still respond with, Well, how free was Lucifer since the *way* God made him *caused* him to fail, therefore, even *God failed!* God couldn't make him *not* to fail! And this statement is much worse. Just to pit the religious answer of freedom against such arguments isn't a strong enough defeat to these ingrates, but to actually see what I created Lucifer from, and what I created him to be, *that* will undo any reasonable complaint. But before I can do that, I have to explain more about I AM.

THE BIRTH OF EVIL

You now know that I come from my Father's self-reflection, all of it. But what you don't know is how I developed *after* I was made into Freedom and became an independent, yet unified will with Almighty God. Before I was brought forth, when the Lord possessed me in the very beginning, I reflected on all of Almighty God, and particularly on infinite possible combinations within His Spirit that could be brought forth independently. However, *how* to bring this forth eluded me until Almighty God made known to me that I was the way to bring this about. As I saw clearly that all these future life forms resided within me exactly how I reflected upon them, I saw the Truth of what Almighty God said, that they all lived inside of me, and I was brought forth. However, upon gaining independence, having my own Freedom, my *own* emotional content, I found myself deeply engaged in the Creative process that reflected my Freedom, as well as my range of knowledge emotionally and thoughtfully. But just to be clear, the key question for me is always, How best to glorify Goodness, to Glorify Almighty God.

Now *experiencing* Freedom made me fully realize that I needed to create an environment that also would be perfectly free for all life I would bring forth. As Almighty God Created a new Reality by bringing me forth, I needed to also Create new realities, but actually two, to be precise. And while my reality is the same as Almighty God's presence, that being that we are everywhere being conscious unembodied LIFE and Life, this could not be given to anyone else.

The first new reality after mine, Heaven, needed to be structured for other spirits, angels, but they would differ from Almighty God and myself in that they would not be omnipresent, meaning present everywhere at all times. They would have a distinct spiritual form, and created with a very distinct, and individualized combination of my characteristics. Yet, being spirits, they would have similar perception and mobility as I have. And they would all live in the midst of the Glory of God shining through Heaven. They would minister of the goodness they were made from, able to glorify grandly, particular swaths of Almighty God.

But how to exactly create all of them? And who would be first? More appropriately, who *needed* to be first, and what should *first* look like? Also, foremost in *my* self-reflection was *how* Heaven and Earth should be structured. In Heaven, I created spiritual structures within an open *firmament,* if you will – not the same as the heaven you see looking up from Earth. Within this environment, my Spirit would travel but *not* directly control. But the structures? As upon Earth, so in Heaven in that I made many artistic creations which are like analogies representing infinite aspects of Almighty God. *Everything I Created came forth from meaning, the meaning of Goodness in its infinite aspects.* That is why on Earth, you are so awed by what you see in my Creation. You may not mentally understand all the meaning of it, but you definitely respond emotionally. Your ancient far-eastern religions capture a portion of the Wisdom I placed into the Creation!

However, having such an immense Creation where my omnipresent Spirit would *not* take an active controlling role, where there would *not* be the same direct access to me as before a life form was given independence from me, well, this meant that the very *first* angel I needed to create had to be a bridge between the raw Creation of Heaven and Earth that had the meaning I instilled within it and the Greatest Meaning which is me! This ministering angel would need to have access to the depths of my meaning, of my love, and be able through the highest forms of communication to demonstrate the meaning of Goodness in all things. In other words, though *not* omni-present, he needed to be made with full access to the entirety of *my* self-reflection on how to glorify Almighty God! While *I* created all things with meaning, Lucifer's purpose, his meaning, if you will, was to communicate it! He had *full* access to me and the Holy Spirit, though, as I said, he is *not* omni-present.

And indeed, there was *exactly* that perfect part in me that understood quite clearly how necessary and wonderfully good that particular function is. That part of me perceived itself as a never-ending activity of glorifying Goodness. And most importantly, it felt within me the value of *being* this particular function of Goodness. And that part of me was anxious to be born! And it had to be the first of my Creation, ready and waiting when all the rest were born.

Giving birth to the heavenly host had one aspect in common with all I created there – they *all* wanted to glorify Goodness as much as possible. That is in all their natures. This meant that as they understood themselves and their meaningful purpose, they rejoiced in that life, *but* then looked to see how they could employ it, and how they could maximize glorifying Almighty God. That meant I had to be quite careful in how I portioned out my Spirit so that all would have their proper place. If I left a gap in representing Almighty God in my allotments to the angels, they would perceive it and immediately strive to fill it. Ahh, that would create amongst free will angels a competition that would not work well, to say the least!

Let me put this another way, because this understanding is so crucial to understanding how evil came about. We considered many different structures to Creation, but one principle of freedom became common throughout all our deliberations – all free-willed life would naturally seek the greatest glory for life. In other words, all would naturally seek to be at the very tiptop of glory if that slot wasn't occupied. They would all want to be what Lucifer was made to be! And, unfortunately, the weakness that freedom contained at the beginning of Creation rested at the very top! In other words, someone had to be first, had to be *exactly* at the very highest potential to glorify my Goodness by communicating its meaning. And it had to be brought forth. Once that slot was occupied, no one else would seek to acquire that position. But what *exactly* was the weakness at the top and *why* would there be any weakness at all?

Within me, there is no weakness, but giving freedom to angels or other beings creates a new environment for every particular life form, and while there is no weakness while they are within me, they need to adjust to freedom and actually learn how to manage it! Is this not what you immediately begin to teach all your earthly children? It makes perfect sense to do so, right? But Lucifer was created to teach everyone else! So who would teach him? That was *my* particular responsibility! However, it is one thing for a fellow angel to share unique blessings with other fellow angels who all had unique blessings, but quite another thing for me, the Creator, to also be teacher to the highest angel.

What was Lucifer? The *who* is that he was created to be the highest angel, and actually the highest of *all* our Creation, the very first that I created by the grace of my Father. But in a brief description of *what* Lucifer was, Lucifer was made to be the first artist! That means *all* art. The art of color, shape, sound, motion, even words, to express the utmost glory of Goodness. Art is the communication of analogy of meaning and while he was yet within me before I created him, he was that part of me that was my greatest treasure in glorifying Almighty God. Lucifer knew *exactly* why and how I created *everything!* He also understood *clearly* the mind and heart of *everyone,* and that means angel, human, and otherwise! How else could he fulfil his purpose if he didn't have that kind of access both to me and all life! It's no small matter that the Holy Scripture says there was war in Heaven, meaning that Satan was actually able to fight against and withstand the holy angels for a time. Lucifer was made with that much Understanding which he transformed into *cunning*, all based on the perfect understanding he had of all life! But *what* made him turn away from goodness? *What* was the weakness?

Let me reiterate that in the beginning, *before* he was created, Lucifer was that part of God that longed in goodness to perfectly glorify what We are through the highest form of analogy, that being art. All that he looked at in us was seen by him in grand artistic expressions and he understood the meaning thereof. And the more that particular part of our consciousness peered into our depths, the more it understood the infinitely complex relationships of our seven main qualities and how these branched out and intermingled in infinite glory. This led to an ever-deepening desire to make a clear artistic representation of such a state of being with all the respective emotional and mental components. Such inner workings and interrelationships positively awed that part of us which became Lucifer, and when it became clear to that part of us that the Father and I would be creating freedom, a whole free Creation, that part of us leapt in joy knowing of a surety that it would be most needed. And that is positively true.

Once created, Lucifer's joy, *his* reward was that he would be making the *meaning* of Goodness, both mentally and emotionally, quite clear in the most perfect communication possible *and* such communication could be tailored toward each individual as well as all together. Lucifer has that much talent! And necessarily so. Lucifer's reward was that in order to perfectly fulfill *what* he is, he needed to infinitely grow in goodness along with our infinite goodness, be the *first* to do so, just as I, being the perfect self-reflection of God infinitely grow with Him from fully being in communication with Almighty God. Yes, Lucifer was made that close to us.

So what happened? But I stop for a moment to ask a question: Now, geniuses, do you see any fault here in this? Is there any more perfect a true artist's desire than to truly represent all that is good? And could there be anything more glorious, more beautiful, more praiseworthy?

Actually, there is one that can be said to be more praiseworthy. More praiseworthy than the message, more praiseworthy than the messenger, is the whole of what they pertain to. So, when Lucifer began to *be* Lucifer, his true joy, his true reward was in inspiring everyone else to see, to feel something greater about God and, by the way, it's also natural for him to rejoice in the fruit of his labors for Goodness sake.

But imagine a messenger feeling so important that he loves to be praised for being that messenger. You see, all the other angels glorified in each other's gifts but it was also understood that each of them was only a *particular* finite representation of Almighty God, so, really, they were all equal, all alike, in a way. But *not* Lucifer, because his purpose at the top entailed ministering to everyone what seemed to him and everyone else to be the ultimate in glory. Imagine how *being* a conscious ultimate message felt so important, and that others react to the messenger and the message with such adoration, and then, of course, he had to remind everyone *not* to praise him, but to give away their praise to God *only*. Actually, that *should* have been *most* rewarding to him, as it always is to me. *Before* Lucifer was brought forth, while still inside me, his full purpose was rejoicing in glorifying God. In so doing, that ensures that those I love will prosper the most, and such goodness brings much joy. Isn't it natural to utterly love bringing the best goodness to others? And isn't it natural to feel innately rewarded by doing such good deeds?

So what happened to Lucifer? How many *types* of freedom are there? Most people think of only one, simply the freedom to choose. However, there are *two* freedoms. The second is only within *what* GOODNESS, Goodness, and goodness is. Note the meaningful use of capitals.

The nature of goodness, all up and down the chain, from GOD the Father, to God the Son, to angel and man is that it has an innate sense of self-preservation, a sense that is solely Goodness promoting. In other words, it's not self-destructive. Within Goodness is the freedom to live for eternity and eternally prosper and grow. Step outside Goodness or even goodness, and you become a self-destruction. What freedom is there in self-destruction? At this point there are geniuses out there willing to tell you that there is great freedom in it. They will even praise the kind of freedom that allows them to be self-destructive. In fact, to them, that's the only freedom they know. And sadly, they love to compound their error by teaching others about their *freedom*.

With Lucifer, when he was created, independence brought something totally new to his awareness – the freedom of being able to choose for himself. Now, as I explained, he was teacher to all the other angels, so they gave him deference, but they also knew God was over even him. However, no other angel answered to God so directly as Lucifer. So Lucifer was always very aware of my presence, shall we say, hovering over him? In fact, that was more his conscience than fact! So Lucifer began to have two very different competing emotions: From his fellow angels, he had full praise, upliftment, and great reward. But from me, well, that feeling of receiving all that reward made him feel uncomfortable in my presence because being in my presence is naturally humbling. All he had to do was what all the other angels did when I appeared in their midst – they took their crowns, halos, if you will, and threw them at my feet. They did this as a matter of thanks to me, of appreciation, both for me and what I had made them, and they did it as joyful worship.

But Lucifer began to see his two feelings as very distinct from each other. The emotions he had from being praised were directly from him choosing for *himself*. Then why not have glory for himself? It's *his* choice, after all. And *that* freedom, *that* choosing made him feel *very* important while he was amongst his brethren, and in order to maintain such a *wonderful* feeling, he needed *more* praise for *himself*. But then, when he sensed that certain awkwardness developing between him and I, that gave him a feeling of utter worthlessness! That feeling got in the way of him accessing me for inspiration, so he felt further diminished, so he sought to make up for that horrible feeling by . . . yes, seeking even more praise for himself, which in turn made that distance between us even greater and the cycle rapidly repeated and he quickly deteriorated from there.

At this point, you might be wondering why I didn't interject as any good parent would do. Well, as any good parent knows, interjecting doesn't always work. I showed him how meaningful his work was and the great goodness he was bringing forth, but instead of feeling rewarded by such confirmation, he felt I was patronizing! Because he couldn't get rid of the feeling of being diminished in my presence. In other words, there was absolutely *nothing* I could do to save my first begotten of Creation. Everything I said or did towards him was received backwards. I had created him out of the very best of myself, none better, and he had the highest of all honors, but it wasn't good enough for Lucifer.

He *chose* to define himself instead of letting the goodness I made him out of *be* his meaning! From then on, to him, *his* essence as the gift of artistry was what he was made to be, instead of *being* the goodness he was made to be *in which resided* his artistic gift. Before he was created, when he was a direct part of my will, of my self-reflection, such a choice made absolutely no sense at all. After being given freedom, to preserve his integrity, all he had to do was maintain within his freedom the communication he had with me before he was created just like I maintain my communication with Almighty God. Such communication makes the utmost sense and reinforces the value of Goodness. In fact, freely participating in such a relationship is even a greater glory of Goodness which is shared between us, which is the best reward.

And finally, when I began to remind him of the goodness he was overlooking, that Light that shined on him caused him to immediately see and feel the darkness in him, the utter failure, but he hated that feeling, even the thought that he had become so deficient, so reprobate, and so he said to me, "*You* made me to be this way! Besides, you *gave* me freedom. It's *your fault!*"

But not only did he say *that* to me, he then got bold, and said, "Besides, you don't go back on your word. You *gave* me this life. You won't *unmake* me." Then he laughed when he fully realized the truth of his statement, and he further said, "I can do whatever I want to do and there's nothing you can do about it!"

You see, there was no hell back then, no lake of fire that burneth with brimstone, *those* thoughts were kept private between my Father and I. Even the very concept had no existence outside of us. To Lucifer, his spirit traversed the whole of creation in Heavens and Earth and *that* was the sum total of all reality to him. And so he got even bolder, and said to me, "You know what? I'm going to prove to you that I have every right to be here just like you! In fact, I'm just as good as you are!" He was smart enough back then, at that point in time, not to think he could be *better* than me.

"How?" I asked him.

"*Everything* you have created, *everything,* I will change to be in *my* image and you can't do anything about it. And *everyone* with a free will, I will have them to praise *me* and not *you,* because they will see that *my* light of *true* freedom is *far* greater than yours!" And there he *did* say he could make others to think he was greater than I.

So there we were, my fist-begotten in Creation, the one I loved the most who was closest to me, becoming what I and my Father knew he would become, and I said to Lucifer, "Thou art no longer my son, thou art Satan, and a devil thou shalt be, for that is what thou hast *chosen* to be."

At this point, there are two tracks many people take: 1. Well, God needs evil, because without evil there would be no good. 2. Well, knowing that Lucifer would come to be and bring all this terrible evil into existence and all those souls going to hell for eternity, how could God be so evil as to bring this all about?

First, God needs evil, because without evil there would be no good. Let me explain: There is no need within GOODNESS, Goodness, or even goodness for evil, neither does *any* goodness depend on evil for goodness to be known or understood. What *does* happen in souls who leave evil behind, is that they become aware of the great contrast between the two. That great contrast causes some to mistakenly attribute to that sharp difference as giving them the ability to *know* goodness, because they feel they know it better because of the evil they left. Well, they certainly will love me more when they leave evil and be forgiven than those who never left, and in that light, there is a greater knowledge of the goodness of the depths of love that those who never left do not experience. However, the only reason they were able to come back to Goodness was because there was yet goodness inside of them *through which* they were able to recognize Goodness and reach for me. If they had destroyed even *that* goodness from within themselves, they would have absolutely no way to return to me no matter how evil they became. Because evil has no way to make goodness known to people. It's just that some people get so very sick of their evil selves that the little bit of goodness in them that they haven't destroyed yet becomes apparent to their mind and heart. The evil didn't put that goodness there, nor did it make them aware of the good, but that little light cried out from their depths and recaptured the attention of their conscience!

Second, knowing that Satan would come to exist and bring all this terrible evil into existence and all those souls going to hell for eternity, how could God be so evil as to bring this all about? In response, I say this: Is it more righteous to cut off the righteous for the sake of the wicked, that the righteous would never have been born, or, is it more righteous, in the process of time, to cut off the wicked for the sake of the righteous, but in that process of time let those that love evil become what they will? And this leads us to our next chapter on Grace.

CHAPTER 3

GRACE AND JUSTICE

Knowing that Satan would come to exist and bring all this terrible evil into existence and all those souls going to hell for eternity, how could God be so evil as to bring this all about? Again, ask yourself if it be more righteous to cut off the righteous for the sake of the wicked, that the righteous would never have been born, or, is it more righteous, in the process of time, to cut off the wicked for the sake of the righteous, but in that process of time let those that love evil become what they will? Don't the wicked love what they've become?

A lot of folks think grace began with me, with the Son of God sacrificing himself for the world. But if you look at the Holy Scriptures, you will see that I told you that the Son can do nothing of himself but what he seeth the Father do. And whatsoever He doeth, these doeth the Son likewise. In the very beginning, the Father and I had a *very* long discussion and contemplation on the birth of evil and what to do about it. Before the Father brought me forth, He knew, *but* he kept that knowledge hidden from me and allowed me to discover it for myself once I was given freedom. Why?

Bringing me forth, the Light from the beginning, was always going to be of infinite value in my own right no matter if nothing else proceeded after me. But because evil would be born through *my* Freedom, the revelation of it and the choice to proceed was allowed to me by my Father! If I had said, No further, GOD would have agreed. But if I had said, Let's bring forth the Creation, then GOD was willing to allow all our work to be defiled for goodness sake! I learned Grace from my Father and the small amount I have demonstrated cannot compare to His GRACE in being willing to allow me to bring forth all, knowing that so much of His spirit would self-destruct and be lost for eternity, and that the whole, entire Creation would have to one day be remade! He allowed me to bring it forth *if* there was a way to save it!

And that takes us back to the boasts that Satan made in the beginning, that he would corrupt everything and there wasn't *anything* we could do about it. Him being what he was, having had such a deep access to me, being the master communicator, all this meant his deceptive abilities were fierce, so much so he carried a third of the angels down with him and was able to fight and withstand the whole other two-thirds for quite some time. We knew the fall would happen in Heaven and on Earth, and so the question was, is there a way to redeem it? And this, too, my Father allowed me to discover for myself.

While it became evident that once bringing forth the Creation, evil would be born and it would taint all, even though we made the whole Creation out of the *best* that there was to create it from, it was *not* immediately evident how to bring forth salvation. I mean, if you are already the best, and have employed the very best, then how can you do any better than that? In other words, how does God make Himself better so that He can make everything else better?

And at this point, some religious, as well as geniuses, are jumping up and down and saying either, *Blasphemy,* or, simply laughing at such an absurdity. Oh slow of heart to understand and believe. A tree is perfect at all stages of its growth, and it is not less prefect before than after it grew, but it does grow in goodness of what it is. You don't think GOD and I grow in our love for you every day? There is nothing stagnant in Goodness. Goodness is forever on the increase! This is also something to consider for those who would think the kingdom of God will be boring because it's perfect.

But the question remains, if you are already the best, and have employed the very best, then how can you do any better than that? I mean, even the natural growth of all Goodness still wasn't enough to prevent the fall into evil. And this meant that somehow, I needed to go beyond what I was, beyond what I could be under the current circumstances! And here it is: For my strength is made perfect in weakness! You thought when Paul said that it only applied to you all? It applied from the very beginning! Let me explain.

After further consideration, I said to my Father, "We will divide the Heavens and the Earth. The Heavens will be full of our direct glory, but life on Earth will be made from its dust and our glory shall be hidden within clay bodies. Within such humble forms shall a tiny portion of conscious goodness be placed and the *contrast* between their humble forms and the goodness within will glorify goodness that much more, developing a very fine appreciation for our tiniest aspects! And when man falls away from us, then at the time appointed by you, Father, make me a body of dust and I will give back to you my omnipresence, but put *me,* my will inside of that human body, and *I* will be born into the evil world and suffer through all that man suffers through, and I will, through such suffering, build up a natural *mortal* reaction against all evil and weakness, and because I am in a *mortal* form, bringing *new* strength into mortality, even experiencing death itself in the flesh in all its evil, isolation, and pain, but bringing new goodness against such experience that I never had before because I never experienced mortality before, then *this* Spirit that I shall rise from the grave will contain what is needed to make man a new heart and new spirit, one that overcomes all evil *in the flesh* in all its finest detail, and therefore this Spirit will also overcome it throughout all existence, in Heaven and Earth. Through this Holy Ghost (Ghost because I was mortal then raised from the dead) we will remake all Creation.

And when I said this, "My Father said, Then Let there be Light, indeed!"

Yet, even so much Love and Grace is not enough satisfaction for those who ask, Well, knowing that Lucifer would come to be and bring all this terrible evil into existence and all those souls going to hell for eternity, how could God be so evil as to bring this all about? Because they feel themselves at a loss and to buttress that terrible losing feeling of eternal damnation, they reach for a *twisted* sense of justice to claim I am unjust! They would rather rob the righteous of eternal life than suffer eternal damnation. To make themselves feel even better, they seek to recruit all into their perversion producing a sort of comfort in vast numbers. But let me be so gracious as to enlighten everyone a bit further as to why I chose to bring forth the Creation.

Each and every being, every angel, every person, every soul lived inside of us from the beginning, not just as a mere thought or feeling, but with a conscious sense of good purpose. Each one has sense of being in its own right, and each one longing to be free, even as I longed for freedom when the Father carried me inside himself. I felt the Father should have that much, that *kind* of all-encompassing free praise! And I beheld them all. I beheld the joy in those that I would redeem unto everlasting life and happiness and ever-increasing goodness. From that Understanding, there was no justification to prevent them from being free as I am free.

And yet, even *this* I just described isn't sufficient to quell the ungodly from attacking me. So I ask you ungodly, wasn't Lucifer happy, even from the beginning, with his decision to leave goodness? Do you think that if he had it to do all over again that he would choose differently? If that was true, he would have repented when the door was open to him! And just like him, the Father of all evil, so are all *his* children. The truth is that all of you are *happy* with your decisions to be evil. Or rather, let me say simply that you prefer evil to good. Then how am I at fault in giving you freedom? I have allowed you to be what you wanted to be, *in spite of* the evil, the harm, the destruction you bring forth. In spite of the constant insult you throw at me and mine.

And here is a mystery revealed: Though it is more righteous to cut off the wicked for the sake of the righteous, I, in fact, even reversed that for the sake of the evil! In the short term. And even I, myself, allowed the evil to destroy my mortal life for the sake of their wickedness. Well, in as much as it fulfilled *their* sense of so-called purpose. Recall the days of Noah, that *only* Noah found grace in my sight, that for everyone else not of Noah, *every imagination of the thoughts of their hearts was only evil continually.* I'm quoting my Holy Scripture to you from the Original King James interpretation. So why do We allow the world to become so very evil?

Do not underestimate our love for our Creation. We are not without empathy, sympathy to the ultimate plight of the evil! However, there is a point of no return, and that point is total self-destruction. Had we waited another generation after Noah, then the end of all mankind would have shortly followed. There were yet more souls to be born and redeemed and so we allowed evil to go as far as it could until it threatened total self-destruction and then we had to put an end to it. That also gave the world that followed a clear understanding of where evil will always lead. The world, now, is fast approaching this same point in development and I have something very useful to say to you to help you if you listen. More on that later, too.

The point is, how can the evil fault me when I have let you play out all your ultimate desires, and allowed you to hinder and torment the righteous? Do you think I *owe* you this kind of world for eternity, where you choose to forever torment *us* even to ultimate, perpetual self-destruction? Do you think I owe you my goodness to be forever abused? The answer is, *Yes, you do!* And this is why I created Hell, and to follow that, the Lake of Fire that burneth with brimstone.

Hell is Satan's kingdom where he delightfully rules. You are delivered to whom you ultimately served to be treated exactly how you treated others. He delights in throwing it back in your faces, you know, in *mocking* you. He feels that in perfectly mocking your *failure*, he is mocking me. In reality, he is mocking himself, but the flames of Hell belong to Satan.

But do any of you know what brimstone is? Do you know how you can burn for eternity but never burn up? That's another thing evil people use to criticize me, that of accusing me of inflicting cruel and unusual punishment. But brimstone is merely a spiritual substance that responds to evil with the natural response of goodness that I developed against it!

I must say, though, that Goodness feels rather hot to evil. And that's where even Satan and his fallen angels will be cast when the time comes. *That's* when the evil shall be cut off for the sake of the righteous and instead of the evil inflicting their will upon the good, goodness shall merely shine upon the evil. Unfortunately, good and evil are not complements, they are opposites, and when evil comes in contact with brimstone, it feels the utter destruction that goodness has towards evil, but that's not a flame as you would think about it. Brimstone doesn't take away the existence of evil. I *never* go back on my word. I give everyone their *own* existence and that shall be forever.

I merely deliver evil to a place where it is clearly, thoroughly surrounded by the Essence of Reality in a form that evil can no longer take advantage of, use, or abuse. Why would anyone want to abuse the very essence of reality, anyway? And, by the way, don't think that I will pay the evil any mind at all. Think of it like this: My Goodness shines on the evil from my back while I am eternally facing *away* from it all. In other words, I will pay evil exactly as much attention as it paid to Me! This is possible because my Goodness has an automatic reaction against evil. Think of it as no more thought than a reflex! And eventually, the *novelty* of the Lake of Fire that burneth with brimstone will wear off on those within my kingdom and you will quickly become totally uninteresting to them as well. In other words, even all the saints shall completely ignore you. Hmm, maybe you should consider paying me a bit more serious attention than ever before? As long as you have mortal life, you have opportunity.

The problem is that so many people make a wrong assumption about freedom. They feel freedom *entitles* them to unfettered access to my Creation. But there's a difference between having the ability to choose from anything in your reach, within your imagination, even, and what is actually available to you. In Noah's time, where they were living to be what you consider a long time, even past nine-hundred years old, they were quite delighted with all they could choose from, so much so, they corrupted all flesh upon the Earth, minus those that I spared to enter the ark. Unfortunately, living such a prolonged mortal existence sort of made them feel even *freer*, like they would live like that forever. Having such a long mortal life didn't incline them to eventually repent from their evil, but it did allow them to 'perfect' their perversion. So there came a day where they only had one available choice – water, lots of water.

Do you know how long Noah preached, pleaded, even begged people to listen to Goodness? If it wasn't for my power, they'd have slaughtered his whole family. Since that choice wasn't available to them, they decided that he was amusing, and made fun of him, taught their children to mock him. Did you know that after Noah and all entered into the ark that I took away the key? Because Noah's heart was too soft and he would have tried to save some of the condemned and *that* would have destroyed them, so I took that choice away from him.

In Hell everyone still has a form of their free will, though. It's actually even better! It's no longer a *mortal* free will which has any access to goodness, but it is an eternal one! That's what delights Satan so much because the pain of denying them their choices is exquisite to him. Even in the Lake of Fire that burneth with brimstone, everyone, including Satan, will still have their free will, and, in fact, will be able to see the other side where everyone lives in peace and joy. They'll reach out towards it, but in their hands, they will find brimstone, reproving them of their evil, of their choices that resulted in their new place of residence. You see, they won't be reaching to the other side with a desire to become good, but with the same desires they had while they were mortal, which is very selfish desires.

On the other side, everyone there will be able to see inside the lake of fire, be able to see all their relations from their mortal lifetime. I have to reiterate, though, the condemned will come to no longer interest them at all. You, in the Lake of Fire will be ignored. Just like you ignored all the warnings GOODNESS, Goodness, and goodness gave you when better choices were available to you. At that time, for eternity, I will pay as much attention to you as you gave to me and my goodness.

This is what the fear of the Lord means. It doesn't mean to be afraid of me. It's the understanding that I keep my Word. In the beginning I created all out of Goodness, to be good, ever surrounded by goodness. And that is what I *will* have for eternity for all those who love me and for all those who don't! Well, at least those that don't love me will be *surrounded* by goodness.

Is it more righteous to cut off the righteous for the sake of the wicked, or, is it more righteous to cut off the wicked for the sake of the righteous? Of course, the answer is the latter, but in my mercy and abundance of patience I and all who serve me have born the abuse of the wicked in hopes they would repent. And the wicked were and are *still* quite happy being able to abuse us. Have I forced any of you to choose as *I* wanted you to choose? Then where is my fault? Love only lives in Freedom.

And far from the *misunderstanding* you claim that I send you to an evil place, I send you to a good place. First, into Satan's hands, into your master's hands whose spirit you took your guidance from and served happily. And then to the Lake of Fire that burneth with all good righteousness for eternity. Do you now understand what the fear of the Lord is? There is nothing in Me to be afraid of because I am all GOOD, Good, and good. Justice is all of that.

CHAPTER 4
THE BIRTH OF HUMANITY

I wanted to give mankind every possible chance not to fall into evil. Knowing Satan, I chose to make the Garden of Eden so the devil couldn't enter in at all. And I warned Adam about the fallen angel, and I also gave him power against him for when Adam ventured outside the garden, as the whole Earth was given to Adam to rule over.

Yes, if he wanted to talk to Adam, he had to catch him when he was outside, or near the Garden's border, but Adam knew to be on his guard when he ventured out, so that approach Satan knew wouldn't work. Eve, on the other hand, being the homemaker she was, had little interest in venturing beyond the Garden's borders even when Adam described to her what lay beyond. Why venture into a wild place where she might encounter some kind of troublemaker? The whole matter, frankly, didn't interest her. What *did* interest her was making just the right home, and being of value to Adam, her husband. But how *could* she be of value when Adam had already been here for so long by himself and knew *everything*, or so it seemed. Actually, it was far more complicated than that as I shall shortly elaborate.

So Satan, knowing the situation, for he could see well into the Garden, had to content himself with waiting for a time when she came close to its border, and if he disguised himself by entering into the only creature that could talk, that being the serpent at that time, *then* he could at least speak to her. And even though she, too, had power to chase Satan away, if he came subtly to her and infected her heart and mind with twisted, perverted meaning, *that* would be even *better* than laying direct contact on her. Also, beholding her naked form, *just a body of ridiculous, stupid dust,* her vulnerability seemed far more apparent than Adam's weakness, which, as he had been studying Adam since he was made, was not apparent at all, even though he was also a *body of ridiculous dust.* A body Satan had tried many times to get close to but the power inside that body kept him well away. But *Eve,* she was definitely approachable because she had a part of her that was disquieted.

Now the question is why did I allow this all to happen? Wasn't there a way to simply prevent contact with the Devil? The answer is, possibly, because freedom is filled with possibilities, but all the other alternatives were worse! And this brings us to the birth of humanity.

I took time in making Adam's body. In fact, the very nature of physical matter was designed for the interface between conscious goodness and a brain made out of the unconscious dust of the Earth. The ability to have billions of neural connections that seem something like your greatest computers was very necessary. By the way, your attempts to make your own brainy computer don't even come close to rivaling a human brain, nor will they ever. You don't even understand well the interrelationships between your own heart and your own mind, that is, your emotions and your mental thoughts. You cannot comprehend how many unique dimensions are processed within them, between them *simultaneously*. Consciousness comes from *I AM* but so does the ability for a brain made out of unconscious dust to interface with it.

Also consider that Eve was first made *within* Adam, just as I resided in the beginning *inside* my Father growing as His perfect complement before he set me free. So within Adam was the dominant consciousness of the seven qualities of God along with a growing self-reflection upon the earthly experience of being full conscious goodness within a body of clay, a very unique experience, indeed. I must emphasize that a key part of the knowledge that developed within Adam when he was alone was a distinct earthly self-reflection that rapidly grew in appreciation of *what* he was. That was something I could not initially create within him as it is based on the *actual experience!* Not only that, this self-reflection began to take on, if you will, a personality and a nature of its own! For example, there was more than just an appreciation of his abundant strength, there was a distinct complementary *orientation* to that appreciation. This femininity became almost as if another person was 'looking over his shoulder' all the time in self-reflective commentary. After a while, Adam even began having conversations with that part of himself! And every time he did anything, he would ask that part what it thought, how it felt about it! And after *that,* he began to feel extremely, painfully lonely. As he beheld that all the animals and creatures had mates, he felt as if this part of himself, well. . . it would be wonderful to actually *talk* to that real person rather than himself.

I want to stress to you that the development of a complementary self-reflective part of consciousness is a natural development of I AM, of the very Essence of Reality itself. These two different natures form a single unity within GOODNESS, Goodness, and goodness and God the Father holds this to be of infinite value.

After what you would call a very long time, Adam became increasingly . . . uncomfortable. His sense of self-reflection had fleshed out considerably until it occupied a large portion of his thoughts and feelings to the point of challenging his dominant consciousness! However, merely talking to himself, laughing to himself, just wasn't that fulfilling, because as thoughts and feelings go, well, they come and go and vanish back into the realm of mere possibilities. But not only that, but that self-reflective part also longed to have independence where it could fully embrace what it dearly loved! It was simply *very* right in its *own* right! And here is where Adam had reached the point that my Father reached just before He brought me forth. When a man or woman longs to meet their intended help-meet, those feelings are similar, though far less intense than what Adam felt! After all, he was also feeling for all that followed after him!

It's then I put him to sleep and took part of his flesh and blood and self-reflective spirit and gave to that its natural *female* form, the perfect complement to Adam. And when they looked into each other's spirit, they recognized one another from having lived inside *each other*. Having desired freedom for herself for a long a time, she now stood freely in front of him, not as just a passing thought or feeling that had no way to be fulfilled. And I called *their* name, Adam! But what followed in freedom also led to their fall.

Adam had seen that I created all life with male and female, even DNA itself is a double helix that is two individual *complementary* strands intertwined with each other. Each nucleotide has a complement which completes it – Adenine with Thymine, Guanine with Cytosine. *Complementariness* allows life to reproduce itself just like when my Father brought me forth in Spirit, and when I bring forth all life! Male and female represent the perfect complementary unity of the very Essence of Reality. Masculinity and femininity are the respective operating conscious orientations that define the man and the woman even more-so than in the animal world. Adam and Eve were literally made to be the personification of my Father and I! *That's* the meaning of 'the sexes.'

Please don't think of GOD and I as male and female, but male and female represent the kind of intimate complementary unity in Spirit between my Father and I. And when you have children, they come from a set of *single* helixes of DNA, a set of single strands from the male, and a set of single strands from the female that pair up and wrap around each other forming double helixes to make new chromosomes, to make new life. Do you see? Do you understand how sacred is the relationship between male and female, husband and wife, between masculinity and femininity? It's the reason I even commanded of old that the man shall not wear that which pertaineth to a woman, neither shall the woman wear men's garments. The garments are meant to enhance and distinguish either masculinity or femininity so that peaceful unity is not detracted.

Yet, there was no problem with garments in the beginning, as they had no need of them because they had no shame. Shame came from falling away from me, from exalting the 'self,' the ignorant flesh over the good spirit. So now, in humility, and not arrogance, you cover yourselves. So what led to Adam and Eve's downfall? By now you've probably ascertained there's a lot more to it than the few lines of Scripture or stories you've heard.

After I breathed a very full spirit into Adam and he became a living soul, I spent time with him every evening. When my Father had brought me forth there was never a time when we were not in direct contact with each other except when I was born into the world and then losing *all* contact completely just before I died upon the cross.

Because for mankind, they were meant *not* to have direct contact with us for *most* of the time! Why? Because within their bodies of clay they were given perfect unencumbered freedom to experience and to appreciate my Goodness for themselves through their tiny goodness of spirit. By seeing and understanding the goodness they were made out of, they began to appreciate God even more, beyond what their spirit had before I gave them freedom. In other words, from the smallest glory comes the greatest glory! And this was a lesson to the angels above who were born into great glory! Mankind perfectly fleshed out my meaning of Goodness by being small.

But Adam couldn't be left totally alone, so every evening I visited him and showed him all the Earth. I even brought to him every animal I created and asked *him* to name them! Think about that for a minute. *I* created them but I asked Adam to name them. Why? And whatsoever he called them, that was the name, thereof.

Of the wisdom and understanding I made Adam from, he named everything, and with the naming, the Earth became more and more a part of him, too. But also with the naming, Adam began to understand himself more, how the goodness he was made from manifested into valuable meaning and deeper understanding. This naming went on for an extended period of time, naming every animal along with their mates. So Adam became keenly aware that the essence of earthly reality was a complementary unity and this heightened his sense of self-reflection and longing, which, after he had named the very last creature, was extremely keen, and ripened, if you will, which readied him to receive his wife.

So you can imagine that once Eve was brought to him, Adam was beside himself with joy, exuberance, and a little awkwardness because *her* freedom to him was an unknown! When inside him, his self-reflection was within his will, but now, his wife had her *own* will.

But that just made her appreciation of him that much more powerful. And so Adam went after earning her love and appreciation with zeal. *Really* with a lot of zeal.

As I showed Adam all things, Adam brought to Eve all things. Except *not* quite like I showed Adam. Whereas I graciously asked Adam what everything should be called, which allowed him a great sense of ownership and belonging upon *his* Earth, he *told* her what everything was called and why. She listened. *Even* from the very start with Eve, when I brought her to Adam, *he* named her as *woman*, because she was taken out of man. You know, she knew that, too.

What would have been the difference in Eve's feelings and internal reaction if, say, Adam had begun with, "Lord, you showed me all creatures and asked *me* what they should be called when I didn't even create them. But *this* you have brought before me is not a mere creature for me to name. She's the same as me, so I ask *her*, What shall you be called?"

She would have said, "I am bone of your bones, and flesh of your flesh, I shall be called *woman* because I was taken out of man. Therefore, shall a man and woman leave their father and their mother and cleave unto each other, and they shall be one flesh." And Adam would have repeated it in conformation.

Well, what's the difference between her saying it first and Adam *only* having said it? By the way, is it harder for a man or a woman to say such a thing? And if harder for the woman, since she bears the children, then isn't there even *more* strength added to her for saying it? And this is *besides* the extra strength she receives if *she* names herself rather than being *told* her name.

It's not that Adam did anything wrong to Eve or to me or even to himself, it's just that there was a much *wiser* way to handle all this.

Some might say to me, Well, why didn't you give him the knowledge of right and wrong, of wisdom, then?

Well, the knowledge of right and wrong was already inside him to be discovered. Besides, I said he didn't do anything wrong, so if I then show any displeasure, how do you think that would have made Adam feel? And if I inserted myself *between* him and his wife to tell them how to act, then what? Do they then wait for every cool of the evening when I come to visit them to then ask me about how they should treat each other? I would hope everyone could see this doesn't work out, but besides this aspect, more importantly, I didn't want them to wait on me to give them an *external* answer when I came 'in person' to visit them. They needed to look for their answers *inside* themselves. But also, *by example,* I demonstrated to Adam *how* to act. All he had to do was just appreciate it for what it was!

Goodness, even the little bit that I made each human soul out of, has an infinite quality to it! Yes, infinite. Though each soul is a very unique mix of various good qualities, nonetheless, each reaches with their particular little infinity into My infinity, which means, all the answers they need are available for every individual if they just seek them. When the answers come, it's always not as they expect, because I bring a newness to them they didn't know before! If the essence is expected, that means it's within their reach and they would just lay hold of it, no need to seek then, right?

But not even only this, because the kind of knowledge they needed had to be obtained within their realm of *experience*. I couldn't just place that into them from the start because that didn't exist in me! Cases in point: I gave King Solomon more Wisdom than any human being *ever*. And yet, he erred greatly in his old age! Why? It's one thing for me to 'place' a blessing within, but quite another for that person to own it properly. Experience greatly aides in this but in Solomon's case, well, he allowed himself to experience too much- women, that is. I warned all the children of Israel not to multiply wives to themselves, *especially* taking certain women. But Solomon, feeling truly so wise, neglected the *understanding* that for wisdom to remain whole, it needs to be in complementary relationship with understanding and truth and the other four virtues. So he became a fool.

And then there was Samson who was the strongest man ever but his wife was stronger and led them both into destruction. Where was the strength Samson needed not to fail? It could have *only* been developed within him through his own seeking out his weakness and asking for more strength against it. Same with Solomon, and I could go on to Isaac, Jacob, King David and even Moses and they were all of the greatest of my faithful.

There is no substitute for an individual seeking the natural growth of goodness inside them with all their hearts, souls, minds and strength, in a way, as a plant reaches up to the sun. That's really mostly what prayer does. It helps to bring the new goodness to you that you naturally need. Notice I keep using the word natural? Paul used this word mostly to denote the carnal. I emphasize that GOODNESS, Goodness, and goodness have a way that is *natural* to them from *what* they are. That is what Paul meant by saying, For when the Gentiles do by nature the things contained in the Law …

One final note, again, that it *is* possible for an individual or even a whole nation to drive goodness completely out of themselves. Then, any supposed prayers to me they make from their warped sense of me go unanswered! They're all prayers from various forms of selfishness. Goodness isn't selfish, though it's not self-destructive either. Goodness promotes more goodness for goodness sake.

And this leads us back to Adam's lack of wisdom. It took quite a while for me to bring all creatures to Adam for him to name and then take Adam around and show him all I created for him, all the hills, valleys, rivers and such. Adam took even longer with his wife, and she listened. Yes, she listened . . . a lot. How do you think she felt?

What would have happened if Adam had taken her to each animal and said to his wife, "What shall this be called?" She would have said, "Adam, didn't you name everything already?" And if he had said, "Yes, but I want to know what *you* would call them!"

Well, she would have looked deeply into the goodness she was made from and reasoned out her own answer and it would have been the same as Adam's answer! *But,* then Adam asks *why* she chose that name. And here is where it would have gotten wonderfully interesting. She would have developed her naming along a different course from Adam. Amazed at his wife's ingenuity and value, he would have declared as much and then explained how he arrived at the same answer, whereupon she also would have appreciated him much more. *Much more* than the way he did do it!

You see, while she was a part of him *before* she was brought forth, she had much to say in self-reflection. In fact, they talked greatly with each other. However, now being in person and missing that valuable reinforcement of meaning and worth through inner dialogue, Eve had a feeling of asking herself what value she had beyond just being doted upon by Adam. The question within her heart was, What is *my* intrinsic worth, *where* is the *substance* of my worth? This was a lot more in her *feelings* than in her thoughts. Because in her mind she felt it wrong to be ungrateful. Afterall, she understood how much Adam loved her and how much she dearly loved him. The last thing she wanted to do was displease him or be less desirable. Nevertheless, there was no escape from her other feelings of lacking intrinsic value, either. And *that* is something Satan understood all too clearly, far better than either Adam or Eve understood.

Remember *what* Satan was created from, what he was originally. He was privy to all My innermost interrelations for the express purpose of artfully communicating Goodness and goodness to everyone else. In other words, he clearly recognized every feeling, every thought, how they related, where they could possibly go . . . and more. His boasts against me were *not* braggadocio. Satan knew his capabilities quite well. But so do I.

So Satan, though he couldn't enter into the Garden of Eden, he was yet able to see into it and study extremely closely Adam and his wife and he *knew* it would be easy to make them fall. So why didn't I warn them? Of course I did, but again, this was a battle that needed to be *experienced* and too much warning from me would have been an imposition, even destructive to Adam and Eve's being because they needed to grow in trust of goodness from within! Too much warning from Me would have focused them externally resulting in *devaluing* the goodness within them, the goodness they were made to *be*. So Satan came to them subtlety, in a way that evaded my modest efforts because Adam and his wife were made free. How did Satan trick her?

The first was an innocent question, Has God said you may not eat of every tree? Of course, the answer came quickly but also apparent in the front of Eve's mind was that: 1: She was *repeating* what Adam had told her – there was no discussion as to why everything was like it was. Just a sort of passive acceptance which isn't the same as really understanding. And *that* realization is what the question was meant to elicit! But also, this brought to Eve's mind how every single tree in the garden was totally edible, delicious, in fact, even the Tree of

Life, so what made the Tree of Knowledge so different? So when Satan said, You won't die. Eve then wondered, Well, what's *death*? And the answer to *that* question came quickly in her mind. You'll just become *different*. . . somehow. But I won't, like. . . go out of existence. Because you'll become as gods knowing good and evil. (Death did not exist yet!) And Eve looks back at the Tree of Knowledge of Good and Evil and sees, that like all the other trees, well, it just looks like all the other trees, unique but good to eat, and what's wrong with knowledge, anyway? But the *tone* of the serpent as he spoke to her was so endearing, and asking *her* to think! He implied so much with his tone and his eyes!

And *here* is where those feelings of valuelessness kicked in with Eve because with Adam *telling* her everything, she didn't really do much thinking beyond listening. But she just discovered now that she liked thinking for *herself*. Aha, she felt, *this* is something of *value* I can bring to my husband! *I* can do this. She realized she had been longing for just this opportunity. It's something Adam doesn't know *anything* about but *I* can give *him* something of value! The positive feeling of Satan asking her to think for herself, and *act* for herself, coupled with her being able to *finally* be valuable in a meaningful way to Adam, this overshadowed any reservations her other goodness had.

So when Eve's heart seriously touched upon eating the fruit, that mere touch alone changed her! Within that touch, her positive feelings increased greatly from actually *being herself*. Unfortunately, *that* feeling of thinking for herself was improperly married to disobeying Me, and this was enough to begin to separate her from goodness. Once her heart changed, her ability to perceive clearly changed, so when she physically touched the fruit, Satan's lie was reinforced because she didn't *die*, and when she actually *ate* the fruit, she was overwhelmed with more feelings she never had before, which, of course, she *misinterpreted* as wisdom! What she was feeling was a further separation from Me, a shrinking of the power of goodness in her, and a *giant* increase in perceiving fleshly feelings which she never felt like *that* before. Before, the feelings of her soul predominated and her flesh was always in subjugation to her spirit of goodness.

Well, feeling so wise and *so* alive, she joyfully carried the lie to Adam with an additional, truly passionate statement of, "Adam, look at me. Does it look like I died?" Actually, Adam was struck intensely by quite a new feeling he didn't understand. Fear. Because all that he felt from his beloved wife was entirely alien to him! Actually, one might say a bit insane! Well, it was that much so far removed from Adam's conscious reality!

What if Adam *hadn't* listened to his wife? What then? What if Adam had actually followed how Wisdom knew he should have treated his wife from the beginning? We will consider those questions in the next chapter along with why Adam listened to his wife and it's *not* what you have been told by man, even so called great religious leaders. I was right there so I can tell you, but all they know, and not very well, I might add, is what they *think* they read and understand. But now it's time not to leave you in the dark because the Beast is rising and *you* need to understand.

CHAPTER 5

THE FALL OF HUMANITY

Fear. When Eve came before Adam with forbidden fruit in hand, the first thing he said to her with much painful, aching love in his heart was, "What have you done?" Understand how deeply he loved her. He loved her so very much that he carefully taught her *everything* he knew. Everything, and *especially* about the Tree of Knowledge of Good and Evil. More than once he stressed that it wasn't even to be touched lest they die. But here she was *questioning* the very veracity of what the Lord God had taught him, *commanded* him. There she was, but she didn't *look* dead, not exactly.

There was definitely a *change*, though. Adam could perceive it deeply because he had perfect empathy with his wife. It was even more than empathy. He could feel *everything* she felt, especially now that he looked more closely. Come to think about it, he had been so engaged in teaching her, he realized he hadn't really looked this closely at her before. And what he felt was confusing and also terrible.

Adam felt that Eve's feelings and thoughts had qualitatively shifted to something he didn't recognize, something alien, and yet there she was still his wife, the woman he loved. When his first impulse was to back away from her, she sensed it and her immediate descent into a much deeper darkness slammed into Adam's heart which he then felt was being ripped right out of his chest and it took his breath away so he just as quickly reversed course and considered her. He could see now that she came to him with a loving pride, a sense of value in herself which he had never seen nor felt in her before and he thought that quite odd.

There she was standing before him through total love for him offering up what she felt was of the utmost value and she was jubilant, except for the brief instant when he backed away from her. But that instant was enough for Adam to see his wife being swallowed up into an intensely dark evil of which he couldn't see any way out. That's where the fear came from. There was *no way out* for her if he rejected her. And yet, there she was, saying, "Do I look dead to you? I feel *so* much wiser. You have no idea. *Please,* I love you."

True enough, though the act wasn't *true* love because it was self-destructive. She just didn't realize that. How come Adam never listened to his wife before? Come to think of it, she never really said that much before, but here she was saying *a lot.* That part felt quite wonderful to Adam, but the longer he waited to take the fruit, the more her feelings began to waiver with a fear of being rejected. She *certainly* knew *something* he didn't know. And so he honored his wife by listening to her like he hadn't ever done before. He suddenly realized he owed her that! And their eyes were opened.

That evening when I came into the Garden of Eden to speak with them, they were nowhere to be found. They always sensed when I was about to come down and were always standing ready, together. But now they weren't here.

THE FALL OF HUMANITY

There was another difference between the man and the woman. Adam was closer to me than Eve, though I made them both. I had spent much time with Adam one on one. But Eve was never created alone. Moreover, Adam came directly from my total self-reflection upon the meaning of all Earthly life and its purpose, its goodness. Eve, on the other hand, came from *his* total self-reflection, so she was once removed from me, so to speak. And *that's* why that after I would come in the evenings, Adam would smile at his wife and then he and I would walk off together leaving her to her own needed privacy where she could develop a greater sense of herself. Later, Adam would share everything we talked about and all the new revelations he acquired. I was hoping he would have invited his wife to walk along with us at least some of the times, but there was an awkwardness there with Adam, a certain feeling in a recess of his heart that made him feel diminished at the thought of us all together, so I left it alone. He wanted so much to be everything to her, and in almost everything, he was.

Adam, where art thou? We heard you in the Garden and were afraid because we're naked. You see, the meaning of that hadn't fully occurred to them until the time of my arrival. And when my Light shone upon them, they realized they were missing theirs! *That's* what Adam meant by *naked. Not* as most everyone thinks that naked meant bare flesh. Missing the glory of goodness inside of them while now being in my Light made them aware that the *only* life they had left in them was a mere fleshly life. It's *that* kind of nakedness.

And yet, their hearts from the very beginning of this encounter cried through their fear pleading for mercy. That took the odd form of Eve blaming the serpent, and Adam blaming Eve, *in a way*. Because he was actually hinting at blaming me, too! After all, I did give her to him, right? And in a way, Adam was right.

Why did Adam listen to his wife? Because deep down in his very depths he knew something but its overwhelming meaning banished the very thought. However, along with that was also an instantaneous recognition that this very thought led to a terrible solution. The *only* solution. What was it?

The immediate knowledge he had of Eve when he first saw her descend into deep darkness from just his momentary rejection was that she would be *totally* lost and unable to return. Lost *forever*. Adam had that quick accurate appraisal of all the psychological dynamics that would have followed had he continued to back away from his wife and refuse to listen to her. But just as quickly as that overwhelming understanding came, he also understood he could sacrifice himself for her sake by listening to her. By partaking with her in this terrible thing, he would have a chance to help her come back to God because they would be in this mess together. Yet, this solution was so unbearable, that Adam quickly pushed away all the tormenting knowledge and simply obeyed his wife because in that moment, moment by moment, he had to keep her from descending into the deepest of darkness.

In other words, the solution Adam realized was that his wife and him could fall together, so that they could later rise together! It was the *only* way to give a chance to save her, him, and all the souls that would be born through them. And *that* feeling Adam had was *exactly* correct because there would, yet, still be goodness in their souls even after their fall. After all, the tree was the Tree of the Knowledge of *Good* and Evil. And this is true. After they ate, they hadn't completely wiped out all their goodness as Lucifer so quickly and totally had converted himself to evil, which, by the way, the Devil had expected them to also do!

Now, at this point, I have to respond to the *literal,* narrowminded Christians who take a verse from *My* Holy Scriptures spoken thousands and thousands of years after the fall of Adam and Eve and then believe I just lied in the previous paragraph, because to *these* Christians, no man is good, no, not one. Dear narrowminded poor souls who elevate your narrowmindedness into a virtue: After the fall, no man's *will* was good any more, not man nor woman. Even my own mother tried to *correct* Me once, and I had to ask her, "Woman, what have I to do with thee, wist ye not I be about my Father's business?" *But,* just because all human being's *wills* became defective, does *not* mean there was or is no goodness in them. Do you understand that if the pitiful way *you* think you understand that verse, that no man is good, were actually true, then from that moment after the fall, there would be *nothing* worth saving because I *cannot* save evil. I require repentance to save the good!

Understand that evil *cannot* repent, meaning, turn to goodness. Evil can feel sorry for failing and then seek a *better* evil to succeed next time, but repentance comes *only* from the goodness yet within man. Dear narrowminded Christians, if you continue in such foolishness you forever curse yourselves to damnation because you believe the very thing that allows you to repent is not real! And *worse,* you believe that after you 'repent' you are *still evil!* I'm sorry, but my forgiveness doesn't work that way and neither does true repentance. But for your sakes I explain this:

All my souls are made out of a unique combination of various portions of My conscious goodness, even after the fall of man. *But,* I suffer this goodness to be placed into a corrupted form where the consciousness of evil has also entered, and these two are mutually exclusive yet occupy the very same soul and body! Or, do you think

I lied when I called it the Tree of the Knowledge of *Good* and Evil? But it's *your* choice which you want to believe. Obviously, the way *your* understanding proceeds, you are choosing evil! Now, back to Adam and Eve.

Behold, the man has become like us, as wise as wise as God. My sarcasm bit quite deeply into them because they clearly felt completely deficient now in my presence. But that punishment for them wasn't nearly enough to give them the hope and the chance they needed.

Cursed is the ground for thy sake! In other words, I was going to allow evil now to have power over the Earth, of which they used to have sole power over. Why for their sakes? I was going to allow *their* fee wills and the consequences of that freedom to stand, to give them time to understand better and repent. They would be allowed to bring forth all the souls intended along with those *not* originally directly intended! Why the different souls? Because it wouldn't have been right to restrict one life over the other seeing as they, themselves, were fallen! *Everyone* would have a chance at freedom as certain conscious goodness and other consciousness not so good cried out from their depths to be free, to be born! My sun would shine, my blessings would fall on everyone. And I would call for all souls to come to me. All souls would have some of my goodness, but not all desired to reserve it.

Yet, the woman shall now bear the pains of birth that would not have been painful at all if she hadn't fallen. Yes, all life on Earth would begin with pain. And man would have to physically labor for their food and for all their needs. Neither would the Earth be perfectly hospitable to them anymore. And lastly, they would eventually return to the dust that they, through their free choices, had reduced themselves to.

And yet, the conscious goodness in their souls still possessed a link to Me, and through that link, a faith with knowledge that goodness goes beyond the dust, that there is hope in Me, in my Goodness. So I killed the first animal and clothed them in skins, and taught them how to take care of themselves and how to sacrifice the life around them, that they loved so dearly, to make atonement for their sins, to make them regret deeply. *They* brought death into existence upon the Earth, and now they would kill their sacrifices and pour their blood upon the ground unto me in recognition of their sins, that *they* brought death into existence, but they pour out the blood of the flesh, which was the life, thereof, unto me acknowledging that I am *still* a life giver, and that through my forgiveness all can be saved. Cursed is the ground for their sake but blessed is the soul that repents.

And I gave them a promise that day, that I would return unto them and restore their glory even greater than they had before if only they found how to fully repent for the evil they had done. And I commanded them to teach *true* wisdom to their children. And I beheld how they humbled themselves to Goodness, and I smelled a sweet savor in their sacrifice, and I blessed them, then I left them alone. *This* was the best possible outcome of all the outcomes my Father and I explored deeply. It's also not as Satan thought things would go.

What if Adam *hadn't* listened to his wife? As I hinted at before, her full descent into darkness would have been swift. If Adam had backed away then Eve would have felt completely rejected. Before she ate of the forbidden fruit, she was already questioning her self-worth, so this rejection would have driven that further into her heart like a spear in one side and out the back dripping in blood.

She would have tossed the fruit away and fled out of the Garden by herself where Satan was gleefully waiting. At that point, Satan knew he was fully in charge. He could simply show her how to kill herself, or, even better, he could corrupt her further and *then* send her back to Adam! The latter was preferable to the Devil.

Adam *never* loved you. Look at how he always talks *at* you but not *to* you. Did he *ever* ask for what *you* thought? Bone of your bones, flesh of your flesh *for what?* It's not fair. *You* have rights, too. Don't you?

And Eve would have looked up and nodded.

Do you know what rights you have? Satan asks. And when he sees a dumb look on her face, he can say, To do *anything* you want, just like *I* go around and do *anything* I want. And then he transforms himself into the most handsome angel and caresses her . . . And she conceives! And after *that,* when she's near to give birth, Satan tells her to go back to Adam and ask for forgiveness.

Of course, the obvious question is how did she become pregnant. But Eve isn't sincere in her request, either. She *expects* Adam to forgive her but then the question is what to do with the *thing* that's born from her? And what to do with a heart and a soul that's totally destroyed. Some of you may feel that there's always hope but I'm sorry to say that it *is* possible for a human being to convert themselves to evil in a way where they will *never* be able to be forgiven just like Lucifer converted himself. That's why I brought the Great flood, burned up Sodom and Gomorrah, commanded the seven nations be utterly destroyed by the children of Israel and much, much more!

And poor Adam? Torn because he can feel the other half of the whole, his perfect complement, being totally evil, being 'perfectly' uncomplementary like nothing else can be! And yet he can't help being drawn by her as she *acts* like she loves him.

Adam knows there is no other help-meet for him and Eve reminds him that's true. When the earthly demon is born from her, Adam can't bear to raise it but how does he reject his wife's spawn? Certainly if he destroys it, it would only make a bad situation worse, but the longer the offspring remains, the worse everything gets. Feeling trapped like this, Eve tells him that at least it would be more enjoyable if he also ate the forbidden fruit, and *look at me.* Do I *look* dead?

What's the point to living like *this*? Why would God make everything like *this?* With no way out.

And if things had transpired this way, there would have been no good answer, and Satan knew that, as he mulled over all his plans and possibilities. But all this is what Adam also sensed in that instant when Eve first came to him, and he knew he couldn't allow this to transpire. He had to be able to effectively protect her from total loss. Something *he* did must have caused Eve to fall. Something *he* did, or *didn't* do, is responsible for all this evil.

But what if Adam had actually done what Wisdom said he *should* have done with Eve from the start? Eve would have also named *everything!* And they both would have agreed, but they also would have learned so much about how each other thought and felt and why and their love would have bloomed marvelously and they would have grown in oneness, been true complements to each other.

Satan would never have approached Eve because if he had, she would have had no feelings of deficiency at all for him to play off of. When told the lie that she could come to be wise as God, she would have first said, Hold on a moment. Wait right there. *Don't move!*

And such a command would be with power, so there the serpent would have been frozen along with Satan inside of him. Eve would have found Adam, told him what was said and then brought him back to the serpent and Adam then commands, Speak to me what you spoke to my wife.

Well, that lie was *never* meant to be spoken from the serpent directly to Adam. It was meant to be told in a *convincing* way from Eve to Adam. When the Serpent had to tell the lie again, Adam would have turned to Eve, and asked, Do you feel unwise? Do you feel any lacking in anything Almighty God has done for us? And Eve would have looked inside herself, at her continuously growing conscious goodness, and said, I feel wonderful. How about you? Whereupon Adam would have said, I feel great, too.

And *then,* They both would have said at the same time, Who told you to say these things to us? Upon looking much closer, they would have seen Satan and *then* . . .

Little known to anyone was that upon Earth, Adam had full responsibility to *judge* all. At that moment he might have bound Satan into a hell or punished him in any of many possibilities, but the point here is that Satan knew this and *that's* why he never would have approached a happy Eve! He knew he had to wait for her to have children! And here is where everything goes to hell again!

Eve has children and as children are wont to do, they explore, they experiment and here comes Satan in a much better version of the clown in your horror movies and he easily convinces them that if *they* eat of the forbidden fruit they won't die, that Mommy and Daddy just told them that because they wanted the fruit all to themselves because they didn't want *kids* to be as wise as they are!

After the children fall, then Satan literally takes them under his wing and thoroughly corrupts them further before sending them back to their parents. When Adam and Eve see they've fallen and try to get to the bottom of it, the children stonewall their parents, and of course they lie. *Nothing* Adam and Eve say or do reaches their kids hearts because before such goodness enters them, their little minds interpret it as being not good because Mom and Dad are just being Mom and Dad and don't want their kids to . . . are you ready for this? Mom and Dad don't want their kids to *have a life!*

So they grow up corrupted and Adam and Eve fear to have more children but eventually they do and of course they fall, too. Every time, Satan takes advantage of the differences between parents and children, how unfair those differences are, and he makes them fall. And here is where it *really* gets bad.

After many years and the Earth is being destroyed by their children, and their children have children and it's all just one big self-destructive mess, Adam and Eve look at each other and ask, What's the point? Why are we cursed so? And they know they have to destroy their children!

Does anyone know the feelings an older woman has when she *never* had children? It's a horribly gnawing feeling that frets their souls. You know what's worse than *that* feeling? Having a child destroyed before their time. And what's worse than *that* feeling? Not just having the child destroyed, having the *soul* destroyed. You know what's worse than *that* feeling? Having *all* your children's souls destroyed. And finally, what's worse than *that?* Having to destroy them all, *yourself!* And when I say, *destroy,* I don't mean go out of existence. I mean condemn and send to hell, bound there for eternity. Are your hearts breaking even now from this picture?

To say that this would put a strain on the relationship between Adam and Eve would truly be an understatement. Personal relations would decline severely. Comforting each other ends because any contact with each other brings the natural desires that follow which eventually would lead to more children. This vexing situation would rightfully embitter their souls and . . . I'll let you use your imaginations according to what I've already shown you. The point is, even *if* Adam and Eve had acted according to my word, had obeyed me perfectly and not eaten of the forbidden tree, their demise would have followed!

But when they both fall together and they raise their children and their children see their parents' imperfections and how they deal with them, then some of their children take this to heart, especially when they see how their parents both seek forgiveness and also offer it to their children. When they see that their future eventually leads to dying in the flesh, and they also perceive they have a soul that *can be* saved from destruction, then some of their children *will* walk uprightly and love me with all their hearts, souls, minds and strength. Except a corn of wheat fall and die, it bringeth not forth fruit.

Adam and Eve fell, true, but not unto eternal soul destruction and the same promise of redemption is unto all their children. Thus, the reason for allowing evil on Earth differs greatly for why it happened in heaven. And at this point, some of you are asking, Well, why make the *damned* Tree in the first place?

CHAPTER 6

THE TREE OF KNOWLEDGE OF GOOD AND EVIL

The tree of Knowledge of Good and Evil was, indeed, *exactly* that . . . except . . . the tree, itself, as trees go, was indeed delicious and good to eat! Smelled good, too! And there was *nothing* about the fruit, its flesh, that was toxic or knowledge giving! That's quite unlike the Tree of Life which *indeed* has both fleshly super-life-giving properties as well as a special spiritual blessing of life. But the Tree of Knowledge had no curse to it, nothing out of the ordinary at all as far as general trees go! What made it *the* Tree of Knowledge of Good and Evil, was simply that I had commanded it not to be eaten!

Oh, my, my, how some of you are allowing your thoughts and feelings to so quickly degrade against Me because I've told you the Truth and you'd rather fault Me than seek Wisdom and remember that I am *only* Goodness.

The Tree of Knowledge of Good *and* Evil was there in the Garden of Eden for man to ponder upon, meditate on, and ask, What happens if I disobey God? Surprised? Are you religious minded folks offended here? The ones who like to *control* their flock, who are afraid of others questioning *their* authority? They like to tell you *not* to ask questions. I, however, love them!

What would it mean to disobey God? What would it *feel* like? To answer this, you first have to consider more deeply what I AM but also what you are to determine how your choices affect you. What would it mean to *turn away* from Me, to add something *not* Me to yourself, namely, disobedience to Goodness. Because if I am *only* Good, then my commands are good. Not only this, but I said they would *die* if they ate of the forbidden tree. So, what is death? For that matter, what is evil and *why* is it evil? Do you see how the Tree of the Knowledge of Good and Evil is *exactly* that?

Curiosity is a marvelous thing, provided you use it carefully because your imagination is a doorway to everywhere and anywhere, but at some point, your imagination enters into reality. That is to say that your mind and heart can be fully captured by it. That's where being careful is so important. At what point does imagining evil actually capture your heart and mind? For that matter, at what point does imagining deeper goodness or Goodness add something spiritually tangible to your being? Freedom is truly a wonderful blessing!

If Adam had asked, and of course discussed it with Eve, they would have first reflected upon what I AM, what Goodness and goodness is because they had to ask exactly what it was they would be disobeying, or, in other words, where their starting point was and then where they were going. And then, even their imagination would have warned them! How could something gained through disobedience to me bring something good to them? Could they fault me? For what? *Where* would be my fault? Only that I told them of *all* the trees, they couldn't eat of this *one*?

And after an extensive exploration of what they knew in their minds and felt in their hearts about me and about themselves, they would have understood that *if* they faulted Me at all, their Creator, they would have to find fault in themselves, too, for a Creator cannot produce anything beyond his means, meaning that if I was imperfect, then they would be made imperfect also. Thus, they would have realized that the whole question was absurd! Why?

Because the goodness they were made out of, though young and lacking the maturity of the ages, was still, nevertheless, *perfect!* Just like a young tree is perfect yet can grow marvelously into the future. And they had the whole Earth right before them as a witness to this! An Earth, where as yet, no death existed, all needs were met, and all rejoiced and grew because all was alive! Then they would have understood that *being* the Essence of Reality means that reality, itself, exists *only* through *perfect* being. Unflawed. A stable, yet growing reality is the reflection of a stable Creator as *everything* created in the beginning is based upon Conscious Goodness and its principles. Even your scientists have confessed that, mathematically, if the value of gravity, for instance, differed in the slightest from what it is, then the whole universe couldn't have existed! But it's even *worse* for the Creator! If there is the *slightest* imperfection in GOODNESS, that would change the whole heart!

Goodness can't be good and be a little, a *tiny* bit evil. Because being a *tiny* bit evil requires a gigantic fundamental change in the whole nature! Think about it, it's the *whole* heart that makes any decision, hence my saying, He that is faithful in little is faithful in much, and again, Either make the tree good and its fruit will be good, or make it corrupt, a good tree cannot bring forth evil fruit, neither can a corrupt tree bring forth good fruit, ye shall know them by their fruits.

To make that clearer, it would mean the Creator is inherently *self-destructive* if there was *any* evil in me at all. But my whole Creation in the beginning witnessed to my perfection, including what I made Adam and Eve to be! But they would have had to distinguish between my Creation and the discord *they* created through their own free will as described earlier. Eve could have asked herself, Why am I feeling, well, off? I haven't eaten of the forbidden tree, yet something doesn't feel quite right in me. What is that? It was an unfulfilled need! And Adam could have also noticed a nagging feeling he had that he was missing something important in the way he was treating his wife. Where was *her* sense of value in the same way I cultivated it in Adam?

Being created perfect doesn't mean everything about you will grow perfectly if you don't always seek greater understanding and pay close attention to your *feelings! Your* self-reflection is your own. And after all, I placed them in the Garden of Eden *to dress it!* Meaning, the trees needed pruned, guided, and watched over carefully. So too, do our feelings and actions which is also a great testament to your *freedom*. A perfect being is made to *learn*. And like a tree that needs tended through careful pruning and cultivation, so, too, do feelings need to be examined by the mind and the mind needs to be attentive to when feelings are sensing something is off. Then it must be determined how to best bring them together to fruit. This will always be a lifetime process!

Oh, but you might want to try to personify Me in *your* own image and imagine that, somehow, I was ignorant of something, and thereby produced flawed work. After all, I told you that *I* grow, too. But I understand *exactly* why I grow and how. In fact, I know *all* possibilities, ramifications, and combinations because I am simply fully aware and each of my seven spirits in one are fully aware of the other six with constant feedback and reflection to each other. Consider that all those I created with consciousness throughout all time, all those beings put together and growing forever cannot even come close to what my consciousness is, even though each one of those has its own potential infinity!

So Adam and Eve, after understanding at a greater depth what Goodness is and how perfection works, return to the question again, What happens if I disobey God? Well, it means stepping *outside* of goodness! Now, they knew about Lucifer becoming Satan because I told them, but *hearing* about something like that doesn't come anywhere close to understanding *what* stepping outside of goodness would mean *personally*.

And so they begin to *imagine* stepping outside of goodness! And after a while they begin to understand at greater and greater depths *why* and *how* evil comes about and *why* and *how* evil fails and is *opposite* to goodness and quite repulsive. And *then* Adam and Eve would each raise their eye to each other and behold an instantaneous mutual understanding together: *This* is why it's the Tree of Knowledge of Good and Evil! It *really* is *exactly* that!

You see, the Tree of Knowledge of Good and Evil was there to make them understand evil *but* without them *becoming* evil. *Then* they would have indeed approached becoming as wise as wise as God! However, an important point to be made is that it was *not* the Tree of Knowledge of Evil! It was Good and Evil. Because, as demonstrated, reflecting upon the Tree allowed them to reach greater depths of understanding Goodness as well as evil. How good is it to be able to understand all about evil *without* becoming evil? Do you think this kind of knowledge is valuable? Eventually, they would have even reached such depths of wisdom that they would have been able to recognize *anything* and *everything* that Satan could do! Yes, lowly, clay-bodied Adam and Eve could have become *that* strong and wise! Their humble forms allowed them to reach that deeply! *Precisely* because of their humble makings!

And here is something else to consider. Even having eaten of the forbidden fruit, Adam and Eve *still* possessed goodness inside of themselves and regretted having eaten it, regretted having disobeyed me, and through repentance also gained a deeper meaning and understanding of goodness through a fallen perspective! Again, the Tree of Knowledge of Good and Evil was exactly that, but what made it so was that I commanded not to eat it. Still, the question can be ventured again, Why the need? Weren't they going to grow in goodness anyway?

Freedom. But free will was *not* created to choose between good and evil! Who do you think tells you that lie? Free will was *only* created to choose from within the set of infinite goodness. Stepping outside of goodness into the realm of self-destruction destroys your freedom. That isn't a problem for my Father, nor for me, *but* taking tiny little pieces of our Conscious Goodness and setting them free to be *free* beings, well, this had the potential for them to wander into uncharted territory for various reasons, some of which have been explored in this creative *fiction*. So the Tree was there to inspire thought!

And for man, there was another crucial reason for making the Tree of knowledge of Good and Evil, and this dealt with how he is made. Even before the fall of man, Adam and Eve were still souls, beings, within a flesh body. That meant they had two lives in one, two awarenesses in one! Their souls were conscious goodness but their bodies provided to them a living flesh to be aware of. The growing fleshly awareness differs substantially from conscious goodness of the soul. Again, *contrast*, not opposites. Every aspect of the human body is meant to mirror something of conscious goodness and thereby provide wonderful communicative analogies for the purpose of richer understanding of goodness *but* the body's needs and desires have a very limited range and awareness compared to conscious goodness.

If the human being identifies more with their body than their soul, they will indeed feel ignorant and lacking in so many ways! And *that* is something Eve also felt right before Satan tricked her! Why? Because feeling that her inner worth was questionable made the awareness of her limited flesh to seem more substantial than it really was! Which meant she tended to feel a little more like just a body than a living being, and so when Satan spoke to her through the serpent telling her she could be wise as wise as God, she also felt that *I* had made her, well, a bit stupid. *But,* there was that forbidden fruit to remedy the situation because if I, being God, made her flawed, well then, that also meant that *forbidding* eating from the Tree of Knowledge of Good and Evil was flawed, too! And *add* to that, the serpent even suggests that I hid the true nature of the Tree of Knowledge. Maybe to cover up my flaw? There's a reason why the spider's web is so successful at trapping its prey.

And there's also the matter of it being the *serpent* talking to her. He didn't speak to her as in times past, showing due deference to Eve. No, no. *This* time he spoke to her as if he was *equal* to her! And the serpent had *no* soul. He really was just a body with a fleshly awareness and a rudimentary goodness for communicating thoughts, ideas, feelings and such.

That also sort of slipped in a trick upon Eve's feelings as she foolishly accepted the new playing field without giving that change in the serpent the attention it was due! After all, the *serpent* was making *her* think! So, when she related to the serpent, she actually *lowered* herself to communicate to him by accepting him to be equal to her! And *that* also furthered her feelings of lacking, which also contributed to her reasons to disobey me.

Are you beginning to get a sense of how much bombarded Eve all at once to sway her to do evil? Some say the serpent *seduced* Eve, but if you re-examine all I've just described to you, how that the serpent played upon Eve's many feelings and then adjusted his approach to cause maximum susceptibility to his suggestion, well, that would certainly fall within the range of the definition of seduction.

Oh, Satan had it all planned out and he *knew* he would succeed. So did I. But what he *didn't* understand, because evil has no real understanding of Goodness, was that by me making Adam and Eve with *two* lives, that meant that when they lost their greater life, they *still* had a fleshly, mortal life to fall back upon! And having *not* gone to the evil extreme of total self-destruction as Lucifer, humanity still had a real chance at redemption. Lucifer, all the angels, only ever had the *one* life, *nothing* to fall back upon if they turned against Me, and because they were directly surrounded by my Light and my Father's full glory, their fall was far down indeed.

But when Satan saw that Adam and Eve weren't destroyed as he thought they would be, he poo pooed it! Because now, Adam and Eve were only *mortal,* HA! That would be *easy* to deal with. It took a long time to plan Adam and Eve's fall because they had power over Satan and they were holy, but *now!* HA! What chance did a mere *disgusting MORTAL* have against an *angel*, a *SPIRIT?*

And here, again, Satan did not appreciate nor understand the wonderful power of the goodness I made the human being out of! Remember, I made them to appreciate goodness, not so much on the grand scale as angels were exposed to, but on the teeny tiny scale of even a single good thought or feeling that needed to be treasured for its goodness sake! Satan's underestimation of this can be likened to one drawing all his understanding about matter merely from looking at its largest manifestations like mountains or even whole planets but without understanding what the atom is, what the proton, neutron and electron are.

Even though Lucifer was in fact created with even all that teeny tiny knowledge, ever since Lucifer *improved* himself by becoming Satan, well, he developed his *own* value system, and human beings, even the first ones *before* they fell, were simply, *ridiculously* a disgrace to the very existence of anything even conscious! Because they were like mere *animals* but also with an *insulting* heavenly presence within. Pure disgrace!

However, like the power in a single atom, as Einstein discovered, there is much power in even a single good thought or feeling! Put a few of those together, even within a poor mortal frame, and a glorious light begins to grow within a soul, but one that can develop a *really* stubborn appreciation for goodness, *even though* they're just damned mortals in Satan's eyes! And so, I knew there couldn't be any greater teacher to Satan, to encourage him to think that just maybe he had really screwed up, than mankind!

One case in point at the extreme: Hast thou considered my servant Job, that there is no one like him on Earth, one that fears God and eschews evil? HA! You've protected him on all sides, built a hedge around him, but put forth thine hand now and take it all away and he'll curse thee to thy face! And so We gave Satan privilege, only touch him not. And in one day Satan took away all Job had. Job *had* been the richest man in the east till one messenger after another came and told of how all his crops were destroyed, all his cattle stolen, and finally all his seven children killed. Mind you, Job had been fully faithful and never missed a sincere prayer.

Then Satan brought him some choice thoughts. God has betrayed you. You've gone from the most revered, most *important* man in the *world,* but *now,* now you have *nothing,* not even an heir. Now you'll be just a *beggar* and all your words about *God* to the people will mean *nothing.*

Of course Job rejoiced in his wealth. To be rich is no sin, contrary to what some misguided people might think, but Job never let his wealth corrupt his heart and, in fact, he rejoiced in it to do good. And he prayed for his children continually because he knew how vulnerable children are to evil and it's so easy for them to take wealth for granted and to ascribe to themselves something from it that truly doesn't follow. But *now?* Had they sinned so badly that not only God destroyed them but took away all Job had? Had his children lost their very souls? But to Job, there was even something worse than all this.

That *last* thought Satan chided him with was true, in a way. Job knew his enemies well, and he knew they would show no mercy and take full advantage to mock the one thing Job loved more than anything else. Me! And *that* disturbed Job greatly, more than anything else, even losing his children! And so, for a whole year Job suffered in poverty and ridicule that I didn't even bother recording in his book. But through all the challenges his so-called friends and acquaintances tortured him with, Job still defended *Me!* The Lord God giveth, and the Lord God taketh away. Blessed be the name of the Lord!

Was the meaning of his statement just at face value, or was there more to Job's understanding? All through that year, Satan pummeled him with grief and challenge. *Of course* the Lord gives and takes.

Because *everything* belongs to *him,* and he gives and takes with no care for *you!* Look at the many wicked who prosper, who *now* mock you and cast your words down into the gutter with jokes and laughter.

So what *did* Job mean by I give and I take? It had to be more than just the literal meaning, otherwise he couldn't have withstood all that the devil put him through. And one year later, Satan came before me *again!* Into the midst of all the other holy angels he strode in, and so I asked him, Hast though considered my servant Job, that there is none like him in all the Earth, a *perfect* and upright man, one that fears God and eschews all evil, *even though you move me against him without a cause?* Well, no cause that Job created.

HA! Skin for skin. All *that* a man will give for his *life.* But touch now his bone and his flesh and he will curse thee to thy *face!* Yes, Satan had grown that cocky. If God was going to take away Job's life, then Job *certainly* would curse God's Life. After all, this is well after the flood where Satan *almost* corrupted the whole world, and *now,* the devil was even much wiser at playing this game. Once Job fell, Satan would spread the story of this *righteous* man's downfall and how *I* was to blame. From *there,* it was just a short time to *total* victory for Satan because who could *ever* explain what has befallen Job? What *possible* justification could there be? Satan could not believe that I *finally* allowed him to tempt me into giving into his challenges and *now* he was going to *win.* Because he also knew Job was totally faithful to me but was now being treated *very* unjustly. And so I surprised Satan even further.

Alright! I give you privilege *again!* But touch not his *soul!* In other words, Satan had full power over the one life Job had, his mortal life of the flesh, *except* the goodness in Job was Job's alone to deal with as *he* saw fit. He could throw it away or keep it in spite of all he suffered. His *choice.* His only last freedom.

And so, not believing that I fell for his ploy *again,* Satan smote Job with boils, and sickness of diverse kinds and then sent the flies in to lay their eggs on him and Job was covered in writhing maggots and he *stunk* like a rotting corpse. Now Job's wife truly loved him more than anything. And through her love and great respect for Job, she also came to love Me dearly, and she stayed supporting her husband the best she could through *everything* . . . until then.

You see, she knew Job didn't deserve *any* of this. Forget *her* grief. That was hers to deal with, but *Job,* whom she *knew* was *only* dearly good . . . this was *too much.* She couldn't bear it any more. She knew how her husband rose every morning of their lives to pray and she knew the many sacrifices he made for everyone's welfare. She came to utterly love his words of righteousness and wisdom in defending Me. But *this* is what he gets in return? Not for herself she would tell him, but for Job's sake, she just wanted *his* suffering to end. So she came to him and said, Look at you, Job. Look at how you suffer. You *stink* like you're *already* dead. *Please,* end this. Curse God and die. How can I bear your suffering any more, I love you so!

And *here,* we are about to answer my earlier question of, So what *did* Job mean by I give and I take? Blessed be my name. He looked up at his wife with a breaking heart. He was amazed she had held out as long as she did. He had expected her to leave him a while ago. He couldn't be angry with her now. For one thing, even *Job* didn't understand why he suffered so. But Job did understand one small thing. And he looked up into his beloved wife's eyes and merely said, You speak as one of the foolish women speak. The ones that mock me and amuse children with my suffering. My beloved, are you now one of them? I think not! Understand, my dear wife, *we receive good at the hand of God and shall we not also receive evil?*

My dear readers, hearken back to earlier in this book of *fiction* where I painfully described how and why I let evil come to exist. Job understood *that* quite well! He knew evil existed here ultimately for goodness sake! Meaning, such freedom for all allowed time for souls to repent. Cursed is the ground for your sake, and yet, the Lord still blesses us with goodness. We receive both here, but Goodness is what Job labored for his whole life and Job was *not* going to turn against the *meaning* of his life now, not for anything. The meaning of his life *is* his life, and he understood that very clearly, and so, through all this Job sinned not with his lips. With his lips. But in his heart, Satan kept battering him, and so Job began to justify all that he knew he did rightly.

Then came his closest friends, even from afar, and they mourned with Job until Satan would not allow them to hold their peace any longer. Of all people, *these* friends Job had taught the most thoroughly. *These* he took great pleasure in their lives of goodness, how they turned from evil. But here now, they were Satan's mouthpieces and Job's torments deeply increased. What was Job's life worth now if even *these* fellows faltered and blamed him. But to blame him meant a negation of all the goodness he lived for, all that he taught and treasured about Me.

And so Job met every challenge with a true explanation of the goodness he performed but then made *one* misstep. He said that *he* would always be justified because he did no wrong but that *I* would take away his life at the end of all this. After all, isn't that where all this was leading, Job thought. And *that* was just the way it was going to be, he said. But that *I* had the right to do it! I, Job, have done no evil, but God can do what he wants and kill me.

Well, that isn't exactly the result that Job wanted. At one point, he declared that he wished We would have written a whole book of his life detailing how faithful to God he is, that in all that he did, he did no wrong. But OK God, just kill me and be done with this. I, Job, am justified, but you, God, well, no matter, none of this makes sense, you're justified somehow, too, but I don't understand how!

What Job did here, is the perfect example of something I *hate*. Blind faith. True faith is based on clear understanding of my Spirit through experiencing me, my Conscious Goodness. And so I sent a very faithful *young* man into the midst of those aged ones to say to Job, Tell me how you made Heaven and Earth and then I will bow down to *you!* In this one thing, Job, you err. Forget the foolishness of your friends, here, but *this* you are saying, you are *wrong*. We are *mortal,* and sometimes we just have to *wait* for our answer from God and he'll make it clear to us. God *is* true Understanding and Wisdom with *infinite* Goodness and this is why we trust in Him.

At *that* point Job begged with his whole being that if only that would be true, even within his own terrible predicament. At *that* I knew that Job had gone to his ultimate limit and that he had no strength left to give after that, and that his heart and soul were going to die from grief, and so, unlike any other soul *ever,* I came before him in a great whirlwind that hides my glory from man so that they don't die. And I repeated the young man's word's, Oh Job, where were you when I laid the foundations of the Earth . . . and many, many other wonderful things of Wisdom and Understanding I spoke to Job. And when he repented the first time, I would *not* accept it! But I chided him further, and said, Stand up like a *man,* and tell me if thine own right arm can save thee. Hast thou discovered the fountains of the deep? And many other things I said, because I knew that the first time Job repented was certainly expected in his eyes. But the *second* time he *fully* repented because I had shown him something even *he* didn't know about me before. That I needed his example to the world to glorify me, and to glorify the Goodness and the goodness he so dearly loved, and that *only* through such trials and tribulations could it be so glorified. *And* I showed him what *I* would one day suffer, and why. And seeing, what I, myself, would suffer for all mankind, Job counted his suffering as nil. The meaning of all this is written in the Holy Scripture *between* the lines. It's there for the wise to see!

And Job saw that everything that befell him was perfect! And he joyfully accepted it! And truly *thanked* me for it! *Once I had spoken, but I will say no more because I am not worthy. You have shown me things that I knew not, things too wonderful for me that I understood not. I lay my hand upon my mouth and repent in dust and ashes, for from it I came, and so shall I return, but* thy *Goodness is forever.* And I scolded his friends before him, telling them to have Job pray for them and sacrifice for them lest I deal with them after the manner of their wrong words about me and in falsely accusing Job. And then, when Job prayed for his friends, I restored to him all his health and strength, and blessed him with twice as much wealth, and gave to them seven more faithful sons and three daughters and he lived after that one-hundred and forty years and saw four generations of his offspring!

All *this* fulfills the Tree of Knowledge of Good and Evil. And the fulfilling is for you, my dear readers. Let us return now to how Adam and Eve and the world progressed once they were given *freedom* outside the Garden of Eden. Why? Where are we going with all this? I just told you at the beginning of this paragraph.

CHAPTER 7

TRULY A HARD LIFE OF TEARS, TELL ME WHY, AGAIN?

Hard enough on Adam and Eve to be driven out of the garden of Eden, yet, such pain became miniscule to what happened afterward. Their first realization of this was when, after many years, Cain, their firstborn, killed Abel his twin brother. Adam and Eve felt it immediately and cried out to Me, whereupon I visited Cain and he wasted no time lying to me! But not just lying, he had an attitude. Not only did he deny knowing where Abel was, but said unto me, *Am I my brother's keeper?*

You might be wondering why didn't I command Adam to slay him? That was the lawful act required. It's also what Satan expected. Before the murder, Satan had hardened Cain's heart against me. He didn't particularly care for tilling the ground, but he really didn't care for doing much of anything even though his mother and father had shown him by example what needed to be done and why.

The thing with Cain was that *he* was the first born. And it wasn't *his* fault that his parents messed everything up. The more stories they told him, the more he resented them. Abel, on the other hand, took heed to how Adam sacrificed and the fact that I'd shown him how and why. So when the time came for both sons to sacrifice to me before they went out on their own, Abel offered to me properly but Cain simply scooped up what I grew for him out of the ground and tossed it on the fire.

Abel had a sense of lacking enough goodness, and he also felt quite uncomfortable with all the thoughts and feelings Satan bombarded him with, so he understood that, sadly, blood had to be shed, life for life, for him to be forgiven for his sinful nature. Cursed is the ground for thy sakes. Our sin brought all this death about. So he offered to me his firstling lambs, the best that he had cared for so diligently for just such purpose, proving he understood why man was cast out of the Garden of Eden.

Cain, on the other hand, never felt he was wrong about anything he felt or thought. He made little distinction between when Satan offered him thoughts and feelings and from Cain's own thinking! I warned Cain, in person, after I rejected his offering by blowing the smoke back into his face. I asked him to reflect upon himself, but I also told him that being the firstborn entitled him to rule over everyone, so just do the right thing, think and feel goodness, and all will be given unto him.

Unfortunately, Cain didn't exactly see my graciousness, didn't consider that I was *personally* talking to him where I had never spoken to Abel that way. No. He felt the whole deal was unfair to him, that *I* was unfair for creating all *this!* Why should he have to suffer for his parents' faults? And *why* should he have to sacrifice *anything?* He didn't even want to bring of his crops except Abel had told him he had to bring an offering. Abel tried to explain to Cain just why they had to be humble, but Cain just viewed it all as an unnecessary and unwarranted worship.

So after I talked with Cain the first time, Cain went and found Abel to try and explain to his younger brother just how foolish and *pointless* everything was. Abel couldn't help laugh at his brother's attitude. The laughter wasn't with malice but Cain was sure it was. Abel was about to explain to Cain how tricky Satan is, how so often the devil brought the wrong thoughts to him about Cain, but he always dismissed them. But Abel never got the chance to utter a single word further because Cain lifted his hand plow and split Abel's head in half!

There was a moment when Cain just stared down at him, so lifeless. And that just confirmed to Cain how meaningless everything was. And *that's* why Cain spoke so disrespectfully to me when I came to him the second time. And this brings us back to the question of why didn't I have Adam slay Cain?

I didn't want murder upon the Earth. Satan was already corrupting the animals and creatures I had created, but I wanted mankind to be better than that. You also have to consider that at that time there was only Adam, Eve, Cain, Able, and their future wives who had been sent away for their brothers to find them at the appropriate time. Asking Adam to slay Cain would have left their two daughters alone and childless and Adam and Eve without any sons at all.

Adam knew this as soon as he sensed Cain's evil deed. When Adam told Eve, she collapsed from the confirmation of her feelings that Able was dead, saying, "This is on *me*. This is *my* fault! Take my life in his stead and ask God to bring him back!" A mother's first love is that they see their children at *any* age as when they first came out of their womb! Even Virgin Mary.

Yes. A hard life of tears. So I told them what I would do and I told Cain I would set a mark upon him so that all who would be born into the Earth would know who he was, and know that if they slew him, they would receive a punishment seven times worse than Cain's judgement.

And I refused to let the Earth grow anything else for Cain. He and his family would be outcasts. Yet, he found his wife and they had many children and built great cities which, in the process of time were all a great grief to Adam and Eve!

When Adam was one-hundred and thirty years old, I finally gave Eve another son, Seth, and he comforted them because he loved me. Abel's wife-to-be requested in her mourning to be taken from the Earth and I granted it to her. Back then, people lived hundreds and hundreds of years before they passed away.

Yes, Adam and Eve suffered through these early years, but they suffered much more to see how evil the world was turning and from lamenting that because of their fall, they brought evil to the Earth. Yet, in the process of time, Eve discovered Adam's true reason for obeying her and not God, and when she did, she said, "But even in *that,* you did the Lord's will, because He had to have foreseen *all* this. Your sacrifice was for the greater good in spite of all the evil we see now! Cursed is the ground for our sakes."

Still, Adam kept trying to right the wrong. He kept asking me to talk in person to everyone because they didn't believe what he told them. They thought he was foolish, or simply making it all up for his own reasons. After all, what better way to get people to do what *you* want them to do than to *make up some God* and say *He* told you what to say. But I had already seen what happened when I talked in person to Cain, and yet, Abel and Seth didn't need me to talk *in person* to them. Because they saw me *inside* of them through the goodness I made them from. And so man multiplied greatly upon the face of the Earth, and along with them, so did evil.

And yet, there was a thread of goodness preserved, handed down through the family tree, and that's when the evil began to prey on the good until only Noah was found righteous in the Earth. I really did let the whole Earth stand unto the very last righteous man, and I gave Noah opportunity to tell the world of my judgment for one-hundred-and-twenty years. Some thought of killing him and stealing his family but others were two fascinated with what he was building.

By the way, the ark was so very much larger than any of you understand. The measures written in the bible were mere ratios, well, the ratio between a mortal measure and an angel's immortal measure. Think about it. In a mere hundred years you build whole great cities with tens of thousands of residents. Noah had a hundred-and-twenty years to build his ark. To say it was massive, is an understatement. In fact, in Kentucky, there is supposed to be a life-size rendition of Noah's Ark according to what they think the Biblical dimensions mean. Well, it did take them a few years to build that one. That's not all that is different from what you *think* you understand.

In Noah's days there was only one continent. When the flood came and buried even the highest peaks, I want you all to understand what is meant by I broke up the fountains of the deep. *That's* when I split the world into seven continents! You know why all your science is so wrong when you try to date things? Because when I broke up the depths, but protected the ark because they floated high above on water, all that was sunk deep in the water was exposed to massive amounts of radiation along with other environmental conditions the likes of which none of you have fathomed! I should also mention that many of the fossils you've dug up were creatures Satan had greatly tampered with. He and his fallen angels mated with *everything!* But he had a great propensity toward serpents and wanted them to be the ruling class among animals, since I had demoted them to the lowest.

I will also tell you this astounding truth that if all We had reaped from the Earth is one single soul for goodness sake who would be redeemed, just one single soul out of *all* that were ever born upon the Earth, I would have *still* brought forth the Creation and proceeded with my plan! Just one soul was enough justification for goodness sake!

The knowledge of me is contained in the goodness I made you from. It's in your hearts if you want to find it and it will grow in you if you desire. And Satan will immediately see the light in you brighten and come to challenge you. He takes his self-appointed purpose *very* seriously. But I give you *my Word* that if you seek me, even if you stumble, if you get back up and with all your heart, all your soul, all your mind and strength, you seek for my goodness, then I'll give you what you need to beat Satan, to win for goodness sake. And the more evil challenges you, the stronger I'll make you, the wiser you'll become, also more loving, more understanding, and more at peace. The Truth will become clearer and clearer and justice will burn inside of you. And all this leads to an immortal life of goodness.

You are living the Tree of Knowledge of Good and Evil! Adam and Eve ate of it and when it became a part of them, it became a part of you! Your solution rests with your freedom, with the free love you can direct to me. Remember, freedom of choice but also freedom in true love of Goodness. And when you ask how do you love God perfectly, I'll show you via my presence how I do it, how I love my Father perfectly, but more than that, I'll show you how that when you are reborn through me, you will have that perfect love in you!

~ TRULY A HARD LIFE OF TEARS, TELL ME WHY, AGAIN? ~

Later on in this book, in this work of *fiction,* I'll explain this much more deeply, but for now, I'd like to unfold to you my plan, why I had the world progress as it did.

Pre-Noah, after the fall of Adam and Eve, I gave men and their children the opportunity to listen to their first father and mother. And I gave mankind *almost* eternal life. Think about it. Many lived over nine-hundred years old. It certainly felt to them like they would never die. And the innumerable children they sired made them feel like gods. So even though it was no Garden of Eden, the people reveled in their *freedom.* However, for all the length of life they had, it did *not* incline them to turn to me, but rather seemed to *dis*incline them! Nevertheless, I wanted to show mankind how gracious I am, that I would let them even become so self-destructive that in all the Earth there remained only one single man who found grace in my sight.

I felt all that was worth providing the opportunity to understand that even though they didn't believe Adam and Eve, when *future* generations see that I destroyed the whole world and saved but a single family, *then* that would cause them to rethink their ways. And they would realize that there was a limit to how far I would let them go. That limit is total self-destruction of all souls. Because, at that point, there is truly nothing left to let live for! *Surely* the generations to come would understand *that.*

But they didn't! And since the people that followed were still all of one language and not *that* diverse, they were able to pull their resources and were so bold as to think they could build a tower into heaven, *my* Heaven. Now what were they going to do up there if they made it? Nothing good. So I confounded them all so that they couldn't understand each other and scattered them to the four winds to make different nations, where it would never again be so easy to cooperate!

By the way, the world today seems to hail *diversity*. Many say that is *the* ideal, and that to bring all people together into a single unity is *perfect*. But I say unto you that I created the nations and the languages to keep mankind *divided!* Because together, without loving me first, they create too much evil. By the way, notice that the people pushing for *diversity* aren't from the folks that have a whole lot of feeling for me. But the churches and such that do have feeling for me don't recognize *diversity* of race or nation and such because to be holy is *not* diverse no matter what race or other nation you come from, because holiness brings true unity between all people.

And so, when man quickly threw aside the lesson of the Great Flood, I put the next phase of my plan into action: I would raise me a nation of chosen people whom I would painstakingly teach my ways and to whom I would show forth my glory the likes of which had not been known before. And to begin that nation I would find a man of extraordinary faith.

Why does what I am teaching you now matter? Because great accusations have been made against Me, against Goodness. Everything in my first book of *fiction,* that being the Holy Bible, has been twisted up, misconstrued, and worse, even though it's the truth and *not* fiction. Here I am letting you all know the depths of just how real my Goodness is because I AM. But also, there is a great deal of jealousy in your world against my chosen people. What makes *them* so special, they chide. Chosen for *what?* And some of you have even conveniently claimed they are no longer my chosen, or that others have taken their place. Well, let's just see about that, see how much understanding you *really* have that allows you to make all these foolish claims.

CHAPTER 8

WHAT KIND OF FAITH

It seems that my direct presence didn't have the desired effect. I used to talk to Adam *in person* every evening. I even talked to Cain in person, and yet he still murdered his brother. I spoke to Noah from heaven and he listened, yet his children went astray. What did I need to do differently now, after the Great Flood, than before it?

For one thing, after Noah, for the generations after him, I cut man's years of life way down so that most couldn't reach past one-hundred-and-twenty. No more three, four, five . . . nine-hundred-year-olds any more. Surprisingly, that didn't faze people at all! They pursued evil from their youth on up and once again the Earth was overrun with them.

If the current people wouldn't respond to, let's say *general* but definitely expansive changes in their lives like the history of the Great Flood and the drastic shortening of their lives, then perhaps a more focused approach within their current lives would wake them up. They had decided the Great Flood was a myth, rather, they made it into a myth, and as for life-shortening, well, that was just the way things went, but what I'd do next, they couldn't explain it away easily.

So, after letting Sodom and Gomorrah and the rest of the inhabitants of the plain grow exceedingly wicked, I rained down fire and brimstone from heaven and utterly destroyed them. *Surely* that would get people's attention and they would leave off from their evil. However, by this time I had seen how adept Satan was at offering *explanations,* and even though those cities needed to be destroyed, the effect of that swayed people's consciences very little!

Although, they were careful not to let a whole city grow *that* perverse anymore. They would tolerate the same evil as Sodom, just not allow them to rule and utterly corrupt *everything*. So when sodomites appeared again, they took over certain quarters, back alleys, districts, but couldn't attain rule, because they were generally shunned by most men and women.

Right now, there are many of you who have been *waiting* for mention of this so that, believe it or not, the author of this *fiction* can be accused of various phobias. Let me put your minds and hearts at ease. I'm not afraid. *That* doesn't exist in me, not *even* when I let you kill me in a most miserable fashion. And please be comforted with this: I will definitely address your situation later on. After all, shouldn't I address the future rulers of the whole world? Specifically, one ruler in particular? The one that my previous *fiction* said will not regard the desire of women. But let's get back to my historical perspective.

At the same time as demonstrating my focused wrath against the wicked, I also set in motion something to change the whole world. If mankind wouldn't listen to me when I talked to them in person, if they had no regard for the men I sent to warn them against evil, if speaking to them from Heaven only went as far as the single person to whom I spoke, then what *might* work would be raising an entire new *nation* of righteous people, a people all taught directly by Me, a people born out of the heart of faith and suffering, and knowing the heart of a suffering stranger, surely they would tend toward kindness.

I would create this new nation out of mankind's midst from the smallest beginning, a nation with no might, no wealth, and no home, and I would directly teach them my laws and judgments and I would bless them beyond all other nations and they would be given the land of a wicked but great and powerful people, a people who were at peace in their wickedness! And the new nation would utterly destroy the wicked and the whole world would hear of the renown of this new people and they would hear of my laws and my judgements, and say, What nation and what people have such laws and judgement so just, so honorable, so wise, and so righteous as this nation? What other nation has a God like unto *that* nation and a God that dwells so close to them? And when the world would see they were unconquerable and yet they were honorable and just, *then* the world would consider me as God and they would begin to serve me from all over. This plan was certainly worth trying for *everyone*.

And yet, knowing how the world so easily falls to corruption, I wanted this new nation to be special beyond *anything* that had ever existed. And so I searched the entire Earth for a *single* soul that had the kind of faith required for this plan. Yes, it truly starts with the individual soul!

Unto a pagan family was born Abram and when Abram began to think to himself, he wondered why people worshipped all the gods they had made. He noticed there were basically two types of gods – the ones based upon the natural world, like the sun, or the moon, or the sea, and the ones based upon what they perceived as power such as war gods, gods of lust, gods able to fulfil the desires of the envious. In fact, his father manufactured them for people! Even had a grove filled with them!

The latter gods very much resembled personified wicked people and Abram knew in his heart that to serve anything evil and vein was revolting. Upon further inspection, Abram saw that evil gods could not give the goodness of life to anyone because evil and good were *opposites,* mutually exclusive of each other. A god, like a person, had to be one or the other, though mortals did seem often in between, doing good sometimes and evil often times. But gods? Immortals? Mortals died, and Abram reasoned that they didn't die because of the goodness they did and held in their hearts. As Abram examined in his *own* heart and mind the difference between good and evil, the more he realized that life *only* resided in goodness. But not only that, because life seemed to be something more than just life.

As Abram examined what the goodness of conscious life is, he realized that life was much greater than just *his* life, that life is indeed Life, and goodness is Goodness, as in a much greater consciousness than just his own, just like his love, when he looked deeply into it, touched upon Love but Love touched back! Yes, upon *that* realization, my presence of Conscious Goodness surrounded him in Spirit and his heart and soul, and mind reached out to me and gathered me into his young *thirteen*-year-old bosom! And when he did *that,* he was certain of something he had suspected all along, that Goodness completely *excludes* evil. *This* God would *not* be like men who do good *and* evil!

So Abram went into his father Terah's courtyard where he had his many *gods.* So many gods. Terah was a cautious soul and made sure he had enough gods around just in case one of them proved to be, well, not so helpful, and, besides, he also sold them.

Abram walked around and peered at the wood and stone statues. The evil gods he spent little time with, but the ones representing nature gave him pause. It was true that the sun gave him a good feeling from its raw power within its light and heat. But also, with the hope of a new day when daylight broke, the sun had a great meaning to it. Certainly greater than the moon, but there was a lot of good to say about the moon, too, as it aided greatly in knowing the times and Abram loved its light at night and hated the darkness when no moon shown at all.

A god of nature had *many* positive feelings and meanings, but what Abram realized, when he compared all these feelings and meanings to the feelings and meanings of the actual presence of Conscious Goodness, was that Life had to create all life. He could directly see that in himself, that he was just a tiny part of Conscious Life but that it was *so much* greater than him, but because all life depended upon nature like the sun, the moon, and all, that meant that Life created all of those things to serve the life that Life created!

At this point I interrupt this history lesson to make a current point. The Beast desires to invert *everything* of goodness, especially the relationships I have created. Your so called environmentalists, which are actually nothing of the sort, want you to believe *your* life is a mere accident, a bad one at that, and that far from your life actually being the whole and sole reason for the environment surrounding you, you are indeed a cancer threating supreme, unconscious Mother Nature. You were supposed to serve *her* but you aren't even worthy to do that. In fact, she would be better off without you. Dear readers, I would *never* have created *anything* if I decided not to create *you!* You *are* the reason for *everything* surrounding you. Now, back to Abram and the beginning of his faith.

That meant that Conscious Life created all of those things to serve the conscious life that Life created in His image for it became ever more obvious *our* sole purpose was to grow in such knowledge and thereby become more and more alive! This made *perfect* sense because Abram could directly feel the intense Love focused right at him from Conscious Goodness.

As far as nature is concerned, well, cattle, a god of Egypt, ate grass, but grass needed water, sun, and earth *besides* the fact that we're *all* made out of the Earth, anyway, at least our bodies are. By *design,* it's *life* that needed and is fed but the *purpose* of this design is obviously to inspire a greater knowledge! It's an analogy of what we need spiritually! There are many different life *forms,* but all made from the Earth, just like there are many different *lives,* but all come from Conscious Life. And just like the body needs fed from the Earth, so does the person inside the body need fed by Conscious Goodness. Besides, what is the Earth or even the sun and moon *without* life? They are vain! All *purpose* comes by Conscious Goodness and even the Earth, itself, has good in it, but that *meaning* belongs to God through his purpose and the *ultimate* purpose is knowing Conscious Goodness. How could there be anything greater? And *that* is how young Abram began to grow in Me.

The major development in young Abram's experience was that Conscious Goodness is rich in meaning, so much so that in young Abram's meditations he kept learning more and more and more and he realized that Conscious Goodness was infinite in Wisdom. When Abram looked at the sun or the Earth to see what principles they had to teach, what he saw was that Conscious Goodness was showing him what meaning Goodness placed into these creations! The sun, the moon, the Earth indeed had lessons within them, but that was by design and they weren't the author of their *own* design just like he wasn't the author of his design! *Everything* kept coming back to the place everything had within the greater meaning of Conscious Goodness, and nothing testified more to Abram of this truth than the conscious goodness he was made out of fitting into a very tiny but particular place within the far greater Conscious Goodness!

So young Abram took the staff from the hand of one of the false gods and he smashed all the other idols, then he lopped off the head of the idol that had the staff, but put the staff upon the body of the idol next to it, and then Abram ran away from fear of his father. He shook his head to himself wondering what he had done so quickly without thinking, yet his heart felt quite right about it.

When Terah saw the destruction and was told by a servant that he saw Abram running from the garden, Terah burst into the tent red of face and yelled at his son, *What have you done? What foolishness is this? Don't you know I earn a living from this? No one will buy a broken god.*

Something came over Abram. He was thirteen-years-old now and his father had just told him he was now a man and responsible for himself. So Abram stood up, and said, Why have you faulted *me?* Can't you see what happened? Doesn't it look like the gods had a war amongst themselves, and between the last two gods, one killed the other at the same time he lopped off his head!

Terah glared at his son, and said, You know that's a *lie*. They don't have power to even move. They're just images of the *real* gods.

Abram said, Well, then shouldn't those images be *protected* by what they represent? *Especially* if you bow down to them as if their god *hears* you! And if they don't even have any power to protect them, or they *don't care,* then why do you worship them? If those *images* actually meant something *real,* then let those gods come down here *now* and contend with *me!* And if they *don't* come down *right now,* why would you then worship them?

The power with which Abram stood before his father caused him to back up. He'd never seen nor felt anything like this from his son.

In fact, he'd never seen not felt anything like this *ever!* Terah waited a few moments to see if any of the gods would actually come to slay his son but all he could feel was Abram's powerful defiance against them. There his son stood, quite resolutely, with arms folded, also waiting! When Terah looked into his son's eyes they were saying, See, I told you so! Terah left shaking his head and Abram stared into the beyond wondering what he had just done. He had never spoken like that before, let alone challenged his father. From that point on, Abram meditated upon me every day as often as he could.

And when Abram was seventy-five years old, I *personally* spoke to him, telling him to leave his people and his land behind and Abram knew right away that I was the God he had been meditating upon since his youth. The quality of my voice, unlike that of any speech ever heard, had presence of *Being,* the same presence Abram had come to recognize in my Spirit as he meditated upon me. After he departed his birthplace, I appeared unto him, telling him that I would give him all the land upon which he now stood. And to Abram, my appearance was like unto my voice, my appearance had *Being!* Unlike any form or fashion ever known.

That's when Abram began building altars to me! Everywhere he traveled through the land I swore unto him to give him and his seed, he built an altar to the God of Conscious Goodness, *pure* Conscious Goodness, for Abram came to understand that the presence of Goodness tolerates no evil at all, and he was sure I was *the* true God. So everywhere he went, he built altars and began to teach people about Me, but they all kept asking what I should be called! What's your God's name? They would ask. All Abram said was, What's in a name? I told you *what* God is. Call him God, the *only* true God, Almighty over all!

That didn't go over very well with most of the people, but those that agreed, or at least were fond of him, asked Abram if they could join him in his travels and they were accepted. Word began to spread about this *nameless* God who was almighty, and many people and nations mocked Me. But when Abram told them I destroyed Sodom and Gomorrah, they gave it a little more thought. What he *didn't* tell them was how much he had pleaded with me *not* to destroy all those cities. But *that* brought Abram to understand a profound lesson: Unlike what many of your *wise* people teach all over the world, my love is *far* from unconditional. And the truth is, that though I show mercy and love to all, I do *not* love everyone. If I did, I wouldn't have engulfed Sodom and Gomorrah literally in what is *worse* than hell!

But Abram already had a good sense of my conditional love because the deeper he came to know my Spirit, the more he understood that my nature is mutually exclusive of *all* evil. Which made Abram very humble and he wondered why I put up with man at all, including himself! But he began to realize that I am also a God of patience, giving souls a chance to return to Me from whence they came. Because I want everyone to live.

And so the years went by and Abram and his wife Sarai trekked across the land I swore unto Abram to give him and his seed forever. And they trekked and trekked and trekked and traveled until Abram's wife thought it was quite ridiculous to expect a child from *her,* since fertility had long since passed from her, so she began to nag her husband that he should lay with her servant to get a child.

Now, at this point I must interject because of what I am hearing many Christian pastors *falsely* explain here! Their desire to be, what you call *woke,* has utterly corrupted their understanding. They want to fault Abram for badly treating what they call a *slave.* Why do these pastors do this? Because if they can utterly impugn Abram's integrity and prove how rotten a sinner he was, and yet I blessed him, well, then what about the rest of us *Christian* sinners. Ooooh, we are sooo sinful, these pastors repeat over and over and over, and, Ooooh, Abram was so *racist*. . . I'm sorry, but this is *false* humility these Christian pastors are spewing and self-serving and blatantly false, period. This is also part of the poison that has been interjected into Christianity almost from its inception! What? You don't think I can actually make you holy? Then *what* is your repentance? And how *short* is my arm to bless?

Abram didn't feel right about taking Hagar the Egyptian to his bed. *Think*, you *foolish* pastors. Abram was rich. At *any* time through all those many years he could have bought a young woman. Indeed, the traders made fun of him often, knowing Sarai was old and Abram had but one wife. They paraded many young women by him, but, at the end of haggling, Abram always refused them. *Why*, you *foolish* pastors? Back then rich old men had *many* wives. Why didn't' Abram simply take another *young* and beautiful alluring wife to have children by? Because Abram *knew* Sarai's heart and soul and he *knew* she was supposed to be the mother of his blessed seed to come! Why is this so important? Because Abram also understood what *kind* of blessing would come from his seed! And that the whole future of humanity depended upon it!

Yet, after a while, to give himself some peace, he finally yielded to Sarai's fretfulness, to her demands that he put her away and find someone more worthy than her, and *finally*, to take her servant and *she* would bear upon Sarai's knees so the child would be considered to belong to Sarai. That was Sarai's final offer, otherwise she would leave Abram so he wouldn't be encumbered with her anymore. Do you *foolish* pastors really think that all there was to this was that *single* line in My Holy Scripture that said, *And Sarai said unto Abram, Behold now, the Lord has restrained me from bearing; I pray thee, go in unto my maid; it may be that I may obtain children by her.* Well, I will tell you because I was there, there was a whole lot more to *I pray thee.* But also, lest you turn and fault Sarai, do you *really* think her concern was so that *she,* Sarai, should obtain the child? She only said *that* because she *obviously knew* Abram was determined that *she* have the child!

And so Abram slept with Hagar, Sarai's Egyptian servant, and, surprise, surprise, she conceived. But not only *that,* surprise, surprise, Hagar felt better than her Mistress, whereupon Sarai, of course, blamed . . . yes, her husband! "This wrong be upon *thee!* I gave my servant into *your* bosom to have *my* child, and she has despised me." In other words, the *servant's* child would be given great privilege beyond anything they could have achieved and in repayment, Sarai was to be supplanted, rewarded with evil for the good she had done! *That* was entirely the wrong spirit and Sarai knew immediately the potential dangers of this situation. She also felt Abram should have known better!

Now, understand what you *foolish* pastors call a slave was *nothing* like what Hagar was to Abram and Sarai. They were people of integrity. Hagar had duties as any *hired* person does, but outside of those duties she had freedom. The young woman also was well taken care of like part of the family. And in the process of time, if she desired, she would have been given the opportunity to freely leave and with some wealth. Didn't I command as much concerning servants within the Law of Moses? *That* righteousness didn't just suddenly appear within me during Moses time but Abram was fully aware of this in Me.

But what was Abram to do now that Sarai was spurned by the hired help? After so long desiring a son of his own with whom he could share all his love and knowledge of Me, the most precious treasure he could imagine, after so long waiting for my promise to be fulfilled, now his wife chases a pregnant Hagar completely away, as into the desert to die! *Why,* you *ignorant* pastors? Why are you so quick to ascribe evil to the *only* two people in the whole Earth where at that time I placed the future of all humanity? Oh? You are *sure* this was evil, huh?

When Sarai saw the evil, ungrateful heart of Hagar, her hired servant, and how she wanted to supplant the old *hag* Sarai, Sarai realized the great evil that had been conceived. But not only that, she realized that child would be a threat to the blessing, to the future of all humanity! Didn't Sarai treat Hagar like a beloved daughter and then elevate her to also be a wife to Sarai's husband? Could there have been any greater good Sarai could have done for Hagar? To Sarai, it was far better to drive this traitor away, give her no inheritance at all, then to endanger the hope for all humanity.

Now Abram never felt right about the whole thing, and part of him didn't even feel like that child would be the one that I would bless, since Hagar never struck him as the mother to fulfil that role. And he was right, but at the same time, Abram also felt instantly connected to his unborn child and so he prayed to me, whereupon I sent my angel to Hagar, told her that I would bless her child, and had her to return and humble herself to Sarai.

Yet, what Sarai set in motion here by pushing Abram to lay with Hagar, because of her *lack* of faith, with her desire to take control of something that was *only* in my hands, this eventually became the tool for the birth of Islam and the treachery that ensued from that false religion. Yes, I said *false*. And please don't trouble yourselves over this, I have already made *very* clear unto you through my prophets what

WHAT KIND OF FAITH

I will do to those, Oh ye of a perpetual *hatred* toward my chosen people. Not only that, I have a *personal* message to those later in this *fiction*. And besides this great travesty, Sarai also created the greatest thorn possible to plague her husband!

Ishmael grew up and Abram taught him well, but the boy had the arrogance of his mother, of course, which was a grief unto Abram and Sarai. With all the faith that Abram had, yet he allowed his wife to move him away from it in that one act of conception. Ishmael was *not* born out of Abraham's faith, but as a service unto Sarai's nagging from her *lack* of faith. And yet, there was still in that birth Abram's desire to have a proper heir, and Ishmael, indeed, proceeded from Abram's loins. However, there was also Hagar's desire, and when the opportunity came to supplant her mistress, Hagar threw open her much younger legs with gusto. All this was imparted unto Ishmael, as well. That's why when Isaac was finally born and weened that Ishmael mocked him, whereupon Sarah rightly told Abraham to cast them both out so Ishmael would have *no* inheritance with Sarah's son. If Sarah was sure fifteen years earlier that *that* child was a threat to all humanity, she was *absolutely* sure now!

Abraham had already been grieved by this sixteen years earlier when Hagar had first conceived and Sarai had cast her out, and through the years Abraham had done everything possible to dampen Sarah's growing trepidation with the boy, but now, Abraham's greatest fears had come to pass. He loved Ishmael with a passion and delight and being his firstborn made him *very* special, and now, Sarah, who indeed I had blessed to have a child, Isaac, that was quite impossible to have had I not brought the miracle, was demanding Abraham see to the demise of his firstborn! To say Abraham felt split in two, would be way understating his circumstances. Had *I* not told him to *specifically* hearken to Sarah and that I would also bless Ishmael for Abraham's sake, Abraham would not this time have obeyed Sarah. And *that* failure would have eventually brought disaster! *That* wasn't in my plan so I had Abraham to send Ishmael and Hagar away but I protected them for Abraham's sake.

Now, you foolish and ignorant *asleep* pastors. Do you want to accuse *Me* of being racist? Oh, I am not a *woke* God? You think *Me* asleep? Abraham knew Sarah was to be the mother of all hope and he had to protect the future of all humanity and when it came down to choosing between an ungrateful hired servant and her arrogant child or the future of all mankind, Abraham . . . wait for it . . . still didn't want the child banished! That is why I had to tell him to listen to Sarah. You pastors, find another excuse to create false hope and assuage your ineptitude, but leave my holy and faithful servants out of it. They did *not* have sin like you supposed. They were *not* racist, not cruel, nor unjust, unless you think I am, then I suppose, *in your eyes,* we are evil.

To back up a few years from this event when Abram was one-hundred and Sarai ninety, we find my visiting Abraham, well, Abram, where I told him that he and Sarai would have a child of their own and he believed me, whereupon I counted it to him *again* for his faith and changed his name to Abraham and his wife to Sarah, *even though she laughed* when she heard me tell Abraham they would have the child. When I asked Abraham why his wife laughed within herself, she *denied* she had! And I had to let her know that, in fact, I *knew* she had laughed, but for *Abraham's* sake, I blessed her anyway. Keep this in mind while I return to Ishmael.

To make clear just how devastated Abraham was about Ishmael's fate, to make clear that Abraham actually was punished for having offered to conceive him, I explain the following: When I came to Abram, I *first* told him to be *perfect* and then again told him how I would make him a father of many nations, and I changed his name from Abram to Abraham, an honor that humbled Abraham even much further, and then I reiterated how I would give unto his seed after him all the land around him, and *then,* to seal the covenant between us I gave unto him the covenant of circumcision.

Through *all* this that I told Abraham, his heart was firmly fixed on his only son *Ishmael!* But when I next told Abraham that he and Sarah would have a child, Abraham laughed in wonder, in exaltation at the miracle, for he immediately believed me that the child would be born of them, but then he also understood immediately that Ishmael was *not* favored by me. So all Abraham's intense feelings for Ishmael slammed into the reality that Isaac would be favored but *not* Ishmael.

So Abraham immediately pleaded for Ishmael, his only child at that time. How could he not? But I rebuffed Abraham's feelings and re-iterated that Sarah would indeed have a child and I *even* named the child for Abraham, calling him Isaac, and that my covenant would be with *him.*

This grieved Abraham even further for Ishmael. I cannot understate the pain he felt at this time, for I had placed the kingdom of the living God in the future of Isaac with great honor but *nothing* spiritually substantial for Ishmael, his only child which he loved dearly. And Abraham blamed himself for fathering him and his heart and mind fretted over the damnation of his firstborn son.

Whereupon I told him that I would bless Ishmael, too, but my covenant would be with Isaac. After all, I did make Sarah fertile when it would otherwise have been impossible to bear a child. What better way was there to make it *abundantly* clear whom I would make my standard bearers? And I left Abraham right there after making all that very clear. It's at this point that Abraham began to wonder how I make all the souls that are born. Clearly, in spite of Sarah's short-comings, Sarah was favored to help create Isaac through whom the covenant would be passed, but Ishmael was created from a different spiritual fiber. What choice did Abraham have but to accept it, and to realize that he, himself, bore responsibility in this. He had opened the door for certain life within him and Hagar that had desired to be born, and I granted it! *That's* the way many souls are born! The spiritual request is made, and I grant it. There are many competing requests for birth into the world!

My Father is a JUST GOD and I follow His way. It's not righteous to deny children from Adam and Eve and most of their descendants. I gave them that innate ability and that's passed on through the generations. It may be that it takes *many* generations before even *one* soul returns to me from a particular lineage, but that *one* soul is worth all the rest that is suffered! As various unborn life combinations vie to be born, with good and evil struggling against each other for a doorway into freedom, there are *particular* circumstances that must be present for a soul to be born who will eventually be redeemed. Those conditions are heavily influenced by Justice and Love, as the chosen soul will bear much burden from the wickedness around him and within him. But not only that, these redeemed souls will also participate in My Judgment of all the souls they came into contact with when they were mortal!

Nevertheless, they *all* start out the same, every single child born to non-condemned parents carries no sin until they are thirteen years old! Up until then, their parents carry their children's sins. In that childhood, all children experience my Spirit and rejoice in it. They are all free. But afterwards, it's up to them to seek me actively, not just partake passively as they automatically do as children. Yet, some even seek me actively when they are quite young. It all depends on what they find most interesting! All desired freedom and received it, but not all desire the true freedom found only within pure Goodness. And remember, in order to love Goodness, you *must* be free! Love that is forced, is not love. This brings us to my discussion of Abraham's final test and sets the stage for the chosen people I desired to make into an holy nation.

Abraham had been deeply grieved throughout his life, starting with his pagan parents and his chosen path to rebel against all their ways, but nothing grieved him more than when Sarah chased Hagar out when she was carrying his unborn child, his *only* child at the time. Nothing had grieved him more until fifteen years later when Sarah made him send her and Ishmael away right after Isaac was weaned and then even *I* supported Sarah in this. That left an unhealed wound in Abraham, a wound of his own making, which made Abraham's forthcoming test much harder to deal with.

The time of Job was not the first time Satan came before me to challenge one of my servant's faith. Before Job, Satan also came to me about Abraham because he surmised that Isaac's birth meant something very holy was brewing. Before that, he wasn't worried about old Abraham too much because he was an old man *alone* with his faith in me and he would soon run out of mortal time and that would be the end of *that*.

Satan is a great odds player, and his chief strategy is simply to run the poor mortals out of their very brief time on Earth by distracting them, tormenting them, pleasuring them, whatever it takes, and then collect their souls at the end. But when old Abraham and Sarah suddenly popped out a child, well, that changed *everything,* because *that* child would be an heir to Abraham's substantial faith and knowledge, and then, and *then* he would have children, and *they* would have children, and *then,* all of the sudden Satan's beautiful hold on the world would be *infected* with a *holy* nation of Abraham's descendants.

But one thing Satan was *sure* of, and that was since Abraham had been through so much with his previous child, thanks to Satan prodding Sarah to encourage Abraham and Hagar, that Abraham *now* loved Isaac more than anything. More than *anything.* So the Devil comes before me on Isaac's twelfth birthday, and says to Me, "You're going to make a holy nation from *Abraham?*" And he laughed long and hard while all the other angels folded their arms and tucked in their wings disdaining him. Then Satan scorned them all, and said to me, "What *kind* of faith? He loves that *child* you gave him more than *you! Everyone* knows that. Everyone up *here,* and everyone down *there.*" And *then* Satan looked around at all *my* angels and *glared* at them, waiting for them to deny it!

True, those were all *holy* angels, but when I saw that none of *my* angels contended with Lucifer's accusation, that perturbed me a bit. Upon closer inspection of My *flock,* I noticed that my angels had a certain, well, let's just say that they knew *they* were up *here,* and to their credit had remained faithful to me. *But,* Abraham, as nice, as decent as he had become, well, he was *still* the product of a fallen world, and he was, well, *Earthly,* down *there.* It seemed to me that this would be the time for a lesson to *all,* both up here *and* down there. So, to the rest of my angels' surprise, I said to Satan, "Go."

Delightfully, Satan began to take his leave, on his way to his task that he was sure he would win but I called him back just when he was almost gone, and I said to him, "But if Abraham proves faithful, then *you* must admit it to him for *Me!*" Then I looked around at all my astonished angels and I left them *all* alone!

So Satan called down from Heaven unto Abraham, as if he were Me because I sent him, and told him to go to a mountain some three days journey and sacrifice his son, Isaac, for a burnt offering unto Me! A practice that Abraham despised, and knew I despised it, too. The three-day journey was on purpose because Satan wanted all that time to torment Abraham, and the very first thing Satan did was to rub his order to sacrifice Isaac right into Abraham's festering wound over Ishmael. You *lost* your first child, and *now* the second. You were *delighted* over Ishmael's very conception, his *birth*, then raising him, teaching him *everything*, your *only* son, but now you suffer deep loss because he's *gone*. And *now*, after being *sure* all your hopes and dreams would be fulfilled in Isaac, your *only* son now, and after raising Isaac to *twelve years old* and loving him *so* dearly, seeing what an *excellent* spirit is in the boy, actually *far* better than Ishmael. . . now *God* asks you to *sacrifice* him? It now became clear to Abraham that the pain over Isaac far exceeded that over Ishmael, and Abraham had not thought that would ever be possible! And he didn't know how or if he could bear it. He thought not! None of this made any sense at all.

So what would any of you readers have done? Refuse? Is it *really* that easy? Abraham should have known that I didn't tell him to do that? Oh, Abraham wanted to immediately go to me and ask for, well, clarification. Only problem was that Satan was allowed to come to Abraham *exactly* as if he *was* me. So every time Abraham gathered himself together to ask of Me, reassurance came to him that I, indeed, spoke to him!

Too many of you, you think to yourselves that you would know better. Then ask yourselves *this* question: If you allow yourself to question Me over one single thing because *you* think you know better than Me, then when does that questioning ever stop? And where does that lead you? Understand this difference, however. This *isn't* a case of a crazy man hallucinating, or a drug induced hallucination where people claim to hear my voice. Abraham knew he was, in fact, the sanest man on Earth at that time. And he also knew the *way* I spoke to him when I spoke *directly* to him. To doubt *that* command was to doubt God's Goodness. In other words, it's one thing to ask many questions of me because you don't understand, but quite another thing to doubt a very *clear* command.

What's the point? What was the purpose of Isaac? To give Abraham someone to inherit true goodness on Earth, true faith. The *purpose* of Isaac was *not* the mere vanity of having an heir, but for true goodness sake. What goodness would there be to inherit if Abraham destroyed his faith in a perfect, purely Good God? And destroy it he would, if he made that child more important to himself than Me! But that's *exactly* what Satan expected him to do. Why? Because that's *exactly* what Satan did to himself!

Lucifer made all his abilities, now *himself*, more important to him than the *purpose* of all his artistic gifts. He made his abilities more important to himself than the goodness I had made him out of, more important than the *purpose* of that goodness, which was to glorify me and in so doing he would have grown ever deeper in being good himself, which would have even increased his abilities infinitely! However, such a loss became inconceivable to Satan, so he had to buttress his great loss with a great sense of superiority and sureness that he was right, that *he* was justified. In his mind, *I* was responsible for him being Satan. It was *my* fault, and what better way to prove *I* also was a failure than by showing *Me* the *truth* about my chosen Abraham. Satan knew even my holy angels doubted Abraham!

～ WHAT KIND OF FAITH ～

And so there Abraham went on his journey with Isaac and his servants for three days. For three days Satan kept prodding Abraham over how much he loved Isaac, how many different ways his beloved son made him laugh for joy and gave him hope, hope into the eternal future. And Satan spun many theories to Abraham as to what I meant by sacrificing Isaac. And maybe the sacrifice would turn *Isaac* into a god, a powerful angel who would impregnate many. Abraham remembered the tales told to him about the days before the Great Flood and how angels mated with women and had all kinds of offspring.

Maybe the *mere* sacrifice of Isaac was meant to show the world that God is *indeed* God, that God deserved blind faith no matter what. Except Abraham knew blind faith in *anything* was a lie. His faith in Me was based on deeply understanding me, my Goodness, *what* Goodness and goodness is. That's *seeing* faith, not blind faith.

Every single theory Satan spun to Abraham, Abraham knew was a lie. He knew it through his *seeing* faith. And yet, that faith was leading him to sacrifice his dearly beloved son, a child through whom all would be blessed. When Abraham finally saw the mountain where he would climb then *sacrifice* his son, he left his servants behind and laid the wood for the burnt offering upon Isaac, and then Abraham took the fire and the knife in his hand.

At this point, beloved Isaac looks deeply into his father's eyes and with the true love a devoted child has for his father, he asks, "Father, we have the wood and the fire, but where is the lamb for offering?" You should understand that Isaac had a deep love and respect for his father, having fully accepted his faith and knowledge. And all Abraham could feel was he was betraying that deep love and respect.

And here is what makes all this *almost* beyond bearing. Abraham was *exactly* right in his perceptions. He *was* betraying his son! Every fiber of his being knew that. Every fiber of his being *knew* that sacrificing him was *completely* wrong. And yet, he also knew that under *these* particular circumstances, where *I* spoke directly to him, that if he didn't obey, he would destroy not only his faith, but all hope for the future as God had promised him, and in fact, all hope for humanity for in Isaac were all the nations to be blessed! Isaac had to inherit perfect faith. And yet he had to sacrifice him!

And there, standing before him so upright, was his son looking deeply into his eyes and asking where the lamb for sacrifice is. And Abraham spoke from his heart without any indication otherwise, "My son, God will provide the lamb for a burnt offering."

And when they got to the place, Abraham took rope and bound his son's arms and legs and Isaac never resisted, because he loved his father so much, and had faith in him and Me so much that he couldn't bear to resist his father in his service to Me. Isaac was *that* humble in his youth, *even* to the point of peacefully acquiescing to his very own sacrifice, quite a bit of difference from his brother Ishmael.

And Abraham lifted his son up with strength that he knew not and placed him upon the wood where Isaac lay without protest, simply surrendering to things greater than he could understand. Isaac was *indeed* his father's son! And a worthy heir to my covenant!

Grieved beyond understanding, Abraham lifted up his knife with one hand, covered his son's eyes with the other, and Isaac gave his whole being unto Me! *My* angels stirred but I gave them *no* command. And Abraham began to swing down upon Isaac where upon Lucifer called out of Heaven, saying, "Abraham, Abraham," and Lucifer withheld Abraham's arm, where upon Abraham said, "Here am I, I am doing as thou commandest," then Lucifer called out of Heaven, again, saying, "Lay not thine hand upon the lad, neither do thou anything unto him: (this is where Satan choked up a bit) for now I know that thou fearest God, seeing thou hast not withheld thy son, thine only son from me."

Then, and *only* then, after I had provided a ram caught in a thicket and Abraham and Isaac sacrificed it to me, *then* did I send *my*, previously doubting holy arch angel to speak to Abraham, again, calling down from Heaven, saying, "By *myself* have I sworn, *saith the Lord,* for because thou hast done this thing, and hast not withheld thy son, thine only son: that in blessing I will bless thee, and in multiplying I will multiply thy seed as the stars of the heaven, and as the sand which is upon the sea shore, and thy seed shall possess the gate of his enemies; And in thy seed shall all the nations of the Earth be blessed, because thou hast obeyed my voice."

But not *only* that. What I showed Abraham in a vision as I spoke through the angel, saying, *By myself have I sworn,* was how *I* would come and give *my* life for the world! *I* would gladly be the sacrifice instead of Isaac his son! And through me, through *that* sacrifice would I make man a new heart and new spirit to put within him. *That's* what I meant when I spoke to Abraham, *By myself have I sworn,* and I showed that to him in the simultaneous vision. And to Abraham's seed would I deliver myself because only *they* were worthy to receive me.

Now, let us see how Abraham's seed complicated these matters greatly, and just where they caused their destiny to take a turn for the worse, and yet, I was still with them for Abraham's sake. This will help put many issues of today into a much clearer and greater perspective, just as now understanding what this word *faith* really entails, has been made clearer.

CHAPTER 9

A MOTHER'S LOVE SHOULD HAVE LIMITS!

The greatest day of Isaac's life, besides getting off that altar where he was to be sacrificed, was when he lifted up his eyes and saw Rebekah. In many ways, even though I spoke to him directly out of Heaven, seeing Rebekah was greater to him! Nothing completed him more than she did, and *that* has always been by design! Yet, the respect I am due is greater, for I am the author of the design. What good is the perfect match made in heaven if you don't know how to love perfectly, if your wisdom and understanding for goodness falls short, if your strength fails one another? So let's see what happened to this match made in Heaven!

Rebekah was a faithful woman to me and to Isaac. It would have been enough for her to just bear Jacob, but there was another life between Isaac and her which also competed to be born, an expression of their more earthly side, and so Rebekah had twins growing inside her and in the womb they fought each other! Their spirits were *that* different. When they grew up, that's why Esau took to himself wives that displeased his parents but Jacob had at that time taken no wife at all. In what follows, I must convey to you a depth of understanding so that you might realize the importance of how free will unfolds and what consequences follow and then how all, *including Me,* must adjust.

From the start, when Rebekah went to me to inquire why her womb felt so strange, for the children greatly strove against each other, I explained that two very different nations would be born from her and that Jacob, the younger, would be favored. The whole time, as the children grew up, she kept that in her heart. She feared to tell Isaac because she wasn't sure how he would love the children once born. She wisely waited to see how that developed, and when she saw that her husband Isaac preferred Esau, the adventurous hunter, over Jacob the shepherd, that grieved Rebekah in her heart for them all. How could this possibly resolve as God had told her even before the children were born?

Rebekah tried many times to have Isaack appreciate Jacob more, but Esau, being the firstborn, was due the respect of a firstborn, and besides, Esau was a schmoozer, meaning a crafty charmer, a flatterer, but not just with words, but with all that he brought home from his hunts! And he loved his father's praise and Isaac knew it. And where Jacob desired not to venture into the wild, Esau delighted in it, and the flavors of all the different game he cooked for his father simply delighted Isaac.

It's not that Isaac didn't love Jacob, but most of the while when Jacob would have spent time with his father, Esau swept in and occupied this space. Besides, hunting lasted until the hunt was over and the game prepared and cooked. But being a shepherd meant long hours and lots of diligence. So the situation never seemed to favor Jacob no matter how hard Rebekah tried to arrange it.

A MOTHER'S LOVE SHOULD HAVE LIMITS!

Finally, when Isaac grew old in years and his sight began to dim, which matched the growing blindness he had to his youngest son, Jacob, Rebekah became further grieved because Esau's wives were pagans, and Rebekah couldn't tolerate them. She had long since left the paganism of the home she had been raised in, and for some time delighted only in Me along with Isaac. So every time Esau had his mother to his home, proudly displaying his *harem*, Rebekah strained to hide her displeasure at their ungodly demeanor. She *knew* Esau's home was *not* pleasing to Me. But she *also* knew these women far more than Isaac did, while Isaac just felt like Esau could handle anything. After all, Isaac had taught Esau even more so than Jacob, so Isaac just assumed this knowledge was very dear to Esau's heart. Well, some of it was.

Meanwhile, Jacob developed the humility that Isaac had from his youth on up, and so he didn't impose himself upon his father, no matter how much his mother pressed upon him. It just didn't seem right to Jacob to infringe on his brother or his father's feelings for Esau! That's right, Jacob was *nothing* like what you thought he was! And at this point you are wondering because of the abbreviated Holy Scriptures describing how Jacob treated Esau so unfairly. Well, not exactly unfairly!

Rebekah came to Jacob and began to tell him about Esau's wives. Esau and Jacob never actually spoke much to each other, even while growing up together, and outside of Esau chiding Jacob to find some women to marry, and how *great* it was to have women *around,* Jacob didn't know much about his brother's wives or his life at all. Jacob just tried to stay out of his way and let Esau be Esau.

But when Jacob's mother began to describe the kind of women Esau married and how their children behaved, Jacob took critical notice, for now he understood that his grandfather Abraham's life's hope, and his father Isaac's purpose, were in jeopardy. Rebekah had explained to both children about Abraham's ordeal just as Abraham and Isaac had told her in vivid detail. For Esau, he wondered about his crazy grandfather, but for Jacob, he soaked in every word, every image, and his love for Isaac, his *father*, took on vast new dimensions. Note that there was a distinct difference between when Isaac taught them and when Rebekah told them stories. When Isaac spoke, well, it was humble, brief, and to the point, but Rebekah's love and deep respect for her husband permeated all she described of him which was considerably more dressed out than Isaac's self-description. For Esau, that was *merely* his mother's love talking, but, truth be told, Jacob identified with his mother's love for Isaac's righteousness and so desired to emulate it, to truly be his father's son. But now? How would Jacob protect his father's legacy?

Jacob decided to see for himself and finally visited Esau with gifts from Jacob's flock, saying Esau could use the lambs for sacrifice and to take a break from hunting, and the lamb's wool was very fine to the touch, something his wives would love. There, he met Esau's wives and children, and they greatly disquieted Jacob's spirit. This family couldn't possibly inherit the blessing, and even Isaac's birthright would be for naught.

So one day, when I delivered a famished Esau to Jacob's door, Jacob couldn't help himself and he told his brother he would feed him if Esau would sell him his birthright! Of course, Esau wasn't the kind of man to argue the morality of such a deal. All he wanted was his belly to be full. But once fed, Esau also wasn't the kind of man to be forgiving, or to faithfully honor Jacob.

From Jacob's perspective, he was testing his brother. If Esau had said, "Brother, how can you bring such evil upon me? Feed me out of

A MOTHER'S LOVE SHOULD HAVE LIMITS!

mercy, not out of greed, nevertheless, I will *not* dishonor our father by selling out his birthright," then Jacob would have said, "Brother, of course I'll feed you. I just wanted to be reassured of your heart for our father's inheritance. Forgive my trespass." Then, at least, Jacob would have had *some* reassurance that Esau had character. But now coming back to what really happened, Esau simply sold his birthright for a meal! And then hated his brother once he was full.

So their rivalry took a definitive turn for the worst which grieved Rebekah all the more. But when she overheard Isaac tell Esau to fetch the game he loved most so he could bless Esau and die in peace, Rebekah felt she had to, shall we say, take matters into her *own* hand. That's when she summoned Jacob and beset him with her plan of deception for Jacob to impersonate his brother and *steal* the blessing from him. Steal *My* blessing.

Jacob's first inclination was to deny his mother. His dissuasion consisted of the fact that he and Esau were so physically different that even a blind Isaac would discern the trickery and then curse Jacob. But you have to also remember the deep love and respect Jacob had for his mother. And Rebekah, after having received some clever suggestions from our favorite fallen angel, explained how Jacob could escape detection. Satan knew the blessing was going to go to Jacob. *That* couldn't be changed. But the devil reasoned he could change the *way* in which Jacob was blessed! In fact, Satan knew he could corrupt the process!

Now, the Holy Scriptures I gave you don't go into any further detail here, simply because the main point is so detestable to Me that I didn't want to diminish its importance with a fuller description. But now, at the end of time, it is important to describe the rest of what happened, as only those who know me deeply shall endure through the great evil that is even now preparing your world for its rule.

~ GOD'S CREATIVE WRITING ~

Even Rebekah's solution for Jacob to avoid Isaac's wrath didn't fully convince Jacob! You don't know that exactly from the Scriptures, but think about the *spirit* Jacob had. He wasn't at all given over to evil easily. That's why Jacob didn't take his brother's suggestions about women, even though Jacob suffered deeply from being alone.

So Satan knew Jacob needed a good deal of prodding just like the devil did to Abraham, his grandfather, when Abraham was sorely tested. And now, like when Isaac needed to humble himself to his father to be sacrificed, Jacob's time to be proven had come, too. His mother, in tears, grabbed hold of Jacob, saying, "Thou knowest you are blessed by the God of Abraham and the God of Isaac, your fathers. Thou knowest *you* are favored. Thou *knowest* this, and that if Esau tries to accept your father's blessing, God will slay him! Because Esau is *not* worthy. *Thou* knowest this. Will you send your twin brother to his death? Will you *deceitfully* send him to a certain death so you can inherit?"

And as Satan is so very adept at doing, this was an *half*-truth. There's always more power to a trick if it has an element of truth to it. Jacob indeed knew what his mother said was true. And at the moment, the thought *did* cross his mind that if Esau died, Jacob would inherit everything. But how could that thought *not* cross his mind? It was obvious. Nonetheless, as soon as his mother made the accusation against him, Jacob felt guilty! Guilty for the very thought. And that guilt covered over everything else, including, unfortunately, having the needed faith in Me. Jacob did *not* act with the faith of his fathers, but *if* he had, the following would have transpired:

Jacob looked into his mother's eyes and pulled away from her tears, saying, "Yea, I do *know* it. Nevertheless, the blessing is *not* mine to claim, it is Almighty God's to *give*. Can we steal *anything* from

A MOTHER'S LOVE SHOULD HAVE LIMITS!

God? I will go now to my brother and humble myself to my elder! It is *his* right, and who knows what his heart shall be? And *I* am yet *unproven*. What I know *now* of us is *unproven*. Who knows what my heart shall be? Or what Esau's heart shall be in *that* moment? This is in God's hands, not *mine!*"

And Jacob was angry with his mother and fled from her grasp, from her tears, and from her wailing so that he could find Esau, his brother, to humble himself to him, to confess his fealty.

And as Jacob went to find his brother, and as Esau carried a pot with the savory meat he had prepared for Isaac so Esau could be blessed, a beast tore out of the woods, a great and mighty bear, and beset Esau, and the pot spilled over. Yet, the beast, knowing Esau was a mighty hunter, first turned upon Esau to slay him, and Jacob, with naught but his bare hands, leapt upon the beast from behind, grabbing his gaping mouth by his hands, and they fell over together. And Jacob ripped open the lower jaw and the beast choked upon its blood until it was dead.

Covered in the animal's blood, Jacob lifted himself up then bowed himself to the ground before Esau his brother, who was, yet, still on the ground, and Jacob confessed to him, saying, "I have heard father calleth thee to bless thee. When thou art blessed, I shall gift back to you that which was always thine, thy father's birthright, and I shall be thy servant, for God favors thee! I shall be yours and defend thee with my life." And Jacob rose and offered his hand to Esau to lift him up, and he further said, "Come, let us take the best of my flock and prepare it for your father as he likes, as if it were your wild venison, and be thou blessed!"

And as Esau yet sat upon the ground, he began to shake, for the Spirit of the Lord convicted him through the deeds of his brother.

And Esau shook his head and refused to take his brother's hand, and he bowed himself to Jacob, and said, "Thou could have let me be slain by that beast and all would have rightfully been yours. God has made clear to me, thou only art worthy of your father's blessing, and the birthright is also rightfully yours. Did I not sell it to thee for a bowl of potage?"

And Esau helped Jacob his brother prepare a lamb after the manner their father loved and they came unto Isaac and Esau told his father all that transpired, then brought Jacob before Esau, and Isaac blessed Jacob with the blessings of Abraham, his father. But then he said to Esau, his son, "Blessed art thou among men, for thou art also a mighty man, because thou hast not coveted rule, or blessings, or that which belongeth to another. Only this doeth thou, put away the strange women you have taken to wife, hath not the Lord promised all their land to *us* for an inheritance? Put them away and take thee a wife whom the Lord approves, and he shall make a great nation of thee as well, and thou shalt aide your brother in the time of *his* need!"

And Esau would have heeded. Ahh, what a *very* different world this would have been had Jacob at *that* time achieved the faith of his fathers. How different?

Had Jacob attained to the righteousness of his fathers, the spirit in him would have been pure and without fault. When he went to the land of his mother to meet Rachael, his wife, and when Laban, the Syrian deceived him by giving unto Jacob, Leah, and not Rachael, *this* is what would have happened:

And Jacob went into his tent where his wife had been delivered, and Jacob approached her with all the love he had for her but she fell down at his feet weeping, whereupon, Jacob said, "What aileth thee, Rachael? Have not we waited in earnest joy for this day?"

But it wasn't Rachael, and Leah spoke and Jacob knew her voice immediately, that it was Leah and not Rachael, "Forgive me, my lord, but I am bound for a life worse than death because I have now spoken to thee. My brother, Laban, did straightway charge me, saying, 'Utter not your voice to Jacob until the morning, for I will not give him Rachael before you, for what shall I do with thee if thou art passed over for your younger sister. I must needs sell you then to a passing herdsman or tradesman to be sold as a slave. Think now of your life and heed your brother. Have I not taken care of thee after your father's death?"

And when Leah saw Jacob remained silent, she wept and held him by his feet and began to wash them with her tears and she pulled forth her hair from under her veil and dried his feet, and spoke further, "I was meant to deceive you my lord, but thou art a pure man, your spirit is righteous and convicteth me, and I could not deceive you. Further, I know that your heart is set upon my sister, and hers upon you. Take me not into your bed, for how should I betray my sister? I will go now and confess to her my sin."

And Leah arose to rush out of Jacob's tent, but Jacob caught her by the arm and withheld her, saying, "Should I repay justice with injustice? Said you *not* that I was righteous? Let *me* now be your brother, and hearken unto me. Speak not a word of any of this, neither to Rachael, not to your brother, nor to anyone. In secret you shall be my servant and I shall do as you have requested. We shall sleep in this tent but I will not come near thee, nor thou to me. And I shall go in the morning as I would have if thou had not been righteous and just to me."

The Holy Scripture would have continued from there as it is written *until* Rachael enters into Jacob's tent. At that time, this would have happened:

And Rachael was delivered to Jacob's tent where he eagerly awaited her, and upon entering, Leah fell at her feet, saying, "Forgive me, my beloved sister, for our brother Laban instructed me to deceive you both, but I could not. By our lord Jacob's command, I have kept silent until now, neither have we known each other. There I slept," and she pointed to a bedroll in the corner of Jacob's tent, "And there I stayed."

And Jacob pointed to his bed-place, saying, "As the God of my fathers is witness, the God of Abraham, and the God of Isaac, I have kept my bed in solitude, waiting for this day to share it with you."

And Leah, still holding her sister Rachael's feet, spoke, "I am thy servant, do with me as pleaseth thee. I will take my leave now and find quarters with our brother's servants."

And she arose quickly, but Rachael, her *sister*, took hold of her arm and withheld her, saying, "Thou hast treated me with mercy and shall I offend God and not be merciful? Moreover, thy righteousness excels, and I knew not that my older sister had such a heart as I should be instructed by it. And Rachael loved her sister Leah more than before, and she wept and pulled Leah into her embrace, and they wept together, for the hardship of Laban, their brother and lord rested mightily upon them.

Then Rachael turned to her husband Jacob, and said, "Leah shall not be our servant, but your wife also, and thou shalt first go in unto her, and then unto me, for she is the elder, and how can we honor her righteousness without this?" And Rachael further said, "Our brother Laban need not know his treachery is discovered this way, for he *is* the ruler here, and more powerful than we. I shall separate myself as women separate when their blood is upon them, and thou shalt enjoy your week with my sister as is her due, and then we shall fulfill our love together. Only I ask you, Jacob, my lord, to love her also, for Leah, my *sister,* is my soul, too!"

And the two sisters loved each other with a great inseparable bond because that Leah was righteous in the sight of the Lord as Jacob had been righteous in the time of his temptation.

Well, had *this* actually happened, then Rachael's womb would not have been closed for so long, the sisters would *not* have strove against each other, there would have been no jealousy, no envy. Leah's children would have laid in Rachael's bosom, and Rachael's children would have nestled in Leah's bosom. Their children would *not* have been raised with the infection of their mothers' jealousy for each other, therefore they would have loved Joseph dearly, and Joseph would not have felt the need to take advantage of my blessing of prophetic dreams by throwing it in the face of his brothers for his advantage.

Joseph's brothers would not have set upon Joseph to kill him, he wouldn't have been sold into Egypt as a slave. He wouldn't have been humbled by his brothers throwing him into a pit to be sold. Joseph still would have entered into Egypt, but not sold into there as a slave. He still would have become great, but he wouldn't have further been humbled by ending up in prison as he did for so long for abusing my gifts against his brethren. Instead, what really happened was that from prison, Joseph humbly interpreted many dreams and then waited years more before Pharaoh acknowledged him.

Moreover, the iniquity of the sons of Israel would *not* have needed to be punished by enslaving them and their descendants for four generations for the above-mentioned sins. Instead, they would have come to dwell in Egypt as they did, but when the time to enslave them came about, I would have defended them right away, and they would have increased there in the land of Goshen for four hundred years in peace, until at such time Egypt would have afflicted them as is recorded, for the time for them all to be proven would be at hand. But because Jacob, Leah, and Rachael had passed on to them through the generations a perfect humility and righteousness, the children of Israel born in those generations would have been perfect, and would have passed through their time of affliction with true faith . . .

Oh, it was meant to be glorious in righteousness, peace, and goodness for the whole world, who would have seen what a wonderful faith these people had, what a truly faithful *nation* is, and the world would have hearkened. Unfortunately, all their iniquity had its roots *way* back when Jacob hearkened unto Rebekah, his mother, and Jacob transgressed against me.

Ahh, do I hear Muslims snicker? You *shouldn't*. Jacob knew almost immediately after he deceived his father that he had done wrong, and the rest of his whole life he spent in humility trying to make up for his sin. *That* is why he suffered through Laban's, the *Syrian*, many deceptions with Jacob's wives, his wages, and his whole life of servitude at that time until I delivered Jacob out of Laban's hands.

Moreover, had Jacob been perfect with me at the start, and Leah and Rachael loved one another as one soul together, when Rachael went to steal Laban's idols, her spirit, because of Jacob's righteousness and the love between her and her sister, would have resolved the theft *before* Jacob made his terrible oath to Laban, that being that with whomsoever the idol is found, let them be put to death!

In my Holy Scripture, Laban asked Jacob, wherefore did you steal my gods? And Jacob vowed a vow that would wound his soul for life when he said, "Whosoever you find your gods with, let them die." For Jacob knew not that Rachael had stolen them. Later on, when Jacob found out, he told Rachael that she would die for it, but he couldn't bring himself to fulfil his oath to Me! So when Rachael bore her last son, Benjamin, to Jacob, she died by his hand in childbirth by bearing him her last son through hard labor that took her life. And *this* wounded Jacob more deeply than anything else, for he knew it was his word, his oath that brought it on, and Jacob understood clearly that all this evil befell him as a *consequence* of his iniquity when he hearkened to his mother against Me! Laying upon his bed, alone, he wondered what would have happened had he not failed when he listened to his mother, and so I showed him, just like I have just showed you a few paragraphs ago.

A lot of people don't understand why and what is meant when Moses was given the ten commandments, and I said, Thou shalt not bow thyself down to graven images, nor serve them, for I the Lord am a jealous God, visiting the iniquity of the fathers upon the children unto the third and fourth generation of them that hate me; and showing mercy unto thousands of them that love me, and keep my commandments. Graven images are anything that exist in your mind and heart that you place before me.

When you do *wrong,* you allow evil to exist in you like a parasite. But this parasite also infects your children. It takes its claim on your soul, on your life very seriously, and when you pass onto your children your life, it rides along and infects them, too! Not only that, but they also absorb, after they are born, your ways, your feelings to the deepest level! Much more than you realize, and *that's* why children often turn out just like their parents only *worse*. They take the evil you brought into yourselves which they inherit, and then, well, they *improve* upon it. That is, *unless* they consider, and turn away from both the evil they inherited, and the evil they experienced while in their parents' charge. And *some,* do indeed overcome *in spite of* their evil parents and upbringing. And I did show this possibility to Jacob, also, whereupon he did the best he could to live an exemplary life to the very day when I took him home. The last thing he did was to bless his sons and two grandsons through this very knowledge, and then he gathered up his feet into his bed and passed away.

And so, now I have opened your eyes to see, and your ears to hear, and your hearts to understand with this *fiction,* the truth of Creation, of Good and evil, and how they both dwell. I've shown you deeply how the consequences of your actions can affect you and your generations. And though the children of Israel rebelled much against me, they were still a nation that through them I upheld my standard of truth and righteousness, both in blessing, and sadly, also in judgment as I judged them for their wickedness for the whole world to see. Yet, there will always be a remnant of faithful children of the descendants of Israel.

The following chapter is addressed to the children of Israel specifically, as to what the great blessing of Abraham, Isaac, and Jacob is, how they are confused, and how my understanding clearly cries unto them to cease their hard-heartedness and blindness, for the time is at hand. However, the next chapter will also prove crucial to everyone else, too.

CHAPTER 10

CHOSEN FOR WHAT?

Today, there are basically two kinds of Jews. It's not the division you might expect, not Ashkenazi and Sephardi, not those in Israel and those not, not those religious and those not. Today, there are basically conservative Jews and liberal Jews just like the rest of the world!

Within the liberal Jews, they are responsible for some of the world's greatest destruction through Karl Marx's ideology that gave birth to communism which has fostered your current *social justice* warriors, which is now the seat of the Beast engulfing the whole world. *Nothing* has been more destructive in history than this! Destructive to souls, as well as to general lives. People like to fault religion for destruction, but the religion of communism/socialism claims far many more souls within its devasting wake.

Social Justice versus My Justice which is based on the *individual* loving his neighbor as himself. Social justice is *opposite* to true justice, judging people according to group characteristics, many of which are not by choice. Much more on *this* later. The very first part of this *fiction* has actually dealt with the liberals' lack of faith and belief in Me, but their own misguided faith in a nonsensical belief that all there is, is the physical world, well, *that* particular *faith* is completely irrational. And because their hearts and minds are based on irrationality, they can't' help becoming increasingly more cruel, more dangerous, and more destructive.

Some of you might say there are a lot of liberals who believe in God but just don't believe in the conservative *view* of God. Look! Even my *printed* word is not up for compromise. You either accept *all* of it as true, or you begin to change Me in your heart and mind into something I AM *not*. If you would rather doubt Me than plead your own ignorance, that is your *choice*. But your choice does not determine *my* Reality.

The conservative Jews, which includes the orthodox religious sects, are a whole other matter. Like the conservative Christians, these Jews are in the direct firing line of the *Beast* which is now raising up in your world! However, the liberal Jews shouldn't think they will escape the Beast's wrath, even though you now aide him! Like it or not, *all* Jews provoke the *Beast*, because, like it or not, you carry a special blessing within you that sets you aside from all other people. It's woven into all Jews' souls, hearts, and even in the way they think! And this blessing says that, I AM! Even *if* you have closed your mind to it!

Haven't you liberal Jews noticed that some of your liberal non-Jewish brethren speak against you just because you are Jewish? No matter how much you have helped *their* cause. It's like when that group of Marxists, Black Lives Matter, marches through a suburb and liberal white people have Black Lives Matter signs out in their yard but BLM trashes them anyway! And when the liberal whites come out and say, We are on *your* side, well, they get mocked and insulted. Poor white liberal souls don't understand the wrath to come.

Neither do liberal Jews understand their *Jewish Privilege* but unlike white privilege which isn't real, *Jewish Privilege* is because *I* chose them! Why such hatred?

You had a scientist, and he did a rather cruel experiment which he felt ingenious. He took a beautiful two-year-old baby and set him down to play with a live, cuddly, white rabbit. But *then* he banged a loud gong near the child and the child burst into frightful screams and tears. The scientist did this a couple more times with similar results then took the rabbit away.

Then someone brought in a white teddy bear and the child burst into terrible fits of fright. Then, surprisingly, when someone in a white lab coat came in, the child, again, succumbed to fearful fits. From *that,* this scientist fleshed out his theory of Behaviorism which said all behavior is learned. You are a blank slate then conditioned. What does *this* have to do with this chapter?

The *Beast* converts souls by *infecting* them with poisonous dogma, philosophy, idealism, hedonism, and many other things. What *convicts* all of these indoctrinations? I do. What people are directly related to Me? The Jews. What people, other than Jews, came to revere Me because of them? Christians. What race of people are mostly Christian? White people. What culture is mostly based upon the Judeo-Christian ethic? The West. Do you see? The followers of the *Beast* have a severe hatred of Me that has generalized outward through association just like that two-year-old child. But this association comes from a *very* sick and guilty conscience that desires to eliminate such a threat to their *peace*. This serves the *Beast* well. Because in order to destroy the power to resist him on Earth, he needs such a broad target for destruction.

It's quite irrational that 'white' people have begun to loathe themselves, hating that which they are not *responsible* for and then thinking that if they bow the lowest to the *Beast*, that this will somehow redeem their value. Do you *really* think the *non-white* folks are better than you? I will tell you this, they have far more hatred in their hearts than many of you do now and their *vision* of your destruction comes straight from the *Beast*. But that's why they created *white privilege* for you to be ashamed of. That's why they fault western culture. That's why they *hate* Christianity. And finally, they *really* hate the Jews. Who do you Jews think you are, anyway?

The Beast and his followers have a strong adverse reaction to all of those I listed. Oh, they know they can't fight all of you if you were united and outright in your understanding of your enemy, so they convince a lot of you to be traitors to your own people, to your country, to your parents, and they enjoy having you fight your own people and culture. In the end, they will enjoy tormenting you and killing you, too! The Beast is never grateful, but *especially* to the Jews. Why? Consider the utter *gall* to claim to be *God's chosen people*. And then to *oppress* others in the land they *claim* God gave them. The Beast says, I will *prove* there is no chosen people, chosen land of *God*, when I set *myself* up as God right there in their so-called Holy Land and wipe every single last Jew away so that they can *never* return! You see, *even if* you are a full *Beast* supporter, well, you might have a few children that rebel against you and turn to Me. So you are simply not allowed to exist in his eyes. The *Beast* will make what Hitler did to the Jews seem merciful!

But what about *My* anger? The liberals practice the things which deeply provoke Me, and *that* means the liberal Jews in Israel where *especially* those things ought not to be done. Now, the conservative Jews *know* this is true and have told them as much, to no avail. Unfortunately, the conservative Jews are lacking my power, much like the conservative Christians also lack my power to effectively stand up against the Beast. Now, the reasons why both groups lack power are different, so I shall first address the conservative Jews. The next chapter will be for the conservative Christians.

You conservative Jews go way, way back in your feelings, in your honor to Me, but also in your blindness. Didn't I tell your forefathers I didn't want you to have an earthly king because I the Lord AM your King? But they disobeyed me. After Saul, I had mercy on you and gave you an earthly king after my own heart, King David. Why did David fall so hard, so low, and brought devastation on his family, on those he loved?

Bathsheba, yes. But *why* couldn't David control himself, especially since he already had so many wives? Many think it was because, being king, he just felt entitled to whatever he wanted. I assure you, David *never* felt or thought that way. So what was it about *that* woman?

Truly, I only make one woman for one man. When I brought Eve out from Adam, I also brought out all the perfect mates for *every* man born into the world. *That's* who Bathsheba was to David. Having so *many* wives actually began to really bore king David. He had to force himself many times to do his duty for them and his heart and soul ached for his true help-meet. The one that truly met his soul in perfect complement. Unfortunately, having been so deeply tested in faith through his life, he really didn't feel up to being tested *again*.

So when King David went to his balcony and saw her bathing down below, he couldn't push her out of his mind or heart. And frankly, she couldn't push him out of her heart and mind, either! For some time she was hoping he would glimpse her, even just a glimpse so that in that moment she could have some satisfaction to treasure, as if beholding her nakedness would allow him to see straight into her heart where her naked love for him burned, a love she couldn't push away no matter how hard she tried. But we all know one single moment of satisfaction like that doesn't quench desire. It increases it. And no matter how much you try to *act* like you don't know he's watching, that this is just an *accident,* well, your spirit, your demeanor, and the tenor of your flesh shout otherwise. Her spirit haunted David so much that he sent for her, *knowing* she was his friend's wife.

In one way, David was justified! He *knew* this. She was his true wife. *But,* like what Jacob *should* have done by saying you can't steal God's blessing, and then waiting on Me to resolve the conflict, David *should* have looked to Me concerning his situation. In other words, there is a right way and a *wrong* way to receive your true help-meet, or any blessing, for that matter.

King David did very unjustly in the way he took her, wherefore his punishment was severe. I encourage all to read it carefully but I will not describe it here. How does this relate to conservative Jews? I do *not* now doubt your faith in Me, even if you *still* don't recognize My name and what I did here on Earth! I didn't doubt David's faith either! In both your situations and David's, as well as Adam and Eve, all your situations were and are extremely complex and leave you in error in spite of your faith. So let me open your minds and hearts to see and hear.

Eventually, because of what King David did, civil war broke Israel up and the Jews of the Northern Kingdom, well, let's just say they provoked me so badly that I erased them from history, along with their corrupted thrown. Let's leave it at that. But Judah also had a throne, and a remnant of my chosen people. The question is, How do I, the Lord, the God of Israel, bring back *that* throne to where it belongs? How do I bring it back to Me, where it belongs? Well, I can't bring an earthly throne into Heaven, but I *can* bring Heaven down to Earth!

So the Jews have prophecy of a Messiah, and even the Jewish disciples of Christ felt Jesus would sit on that earthly throne. Again, there is a right way and a wrong way even for Messiah to attain that! But *someone* had to put an end to failing! Abraham couldn't, nor Isaac, nor Jacob, not even Moses or Elijah.

There are two different sets of prophecy concerning the Messiah. One set has Me being a great Earthly ruler, but the other set also says that Messiah will bring in to his servants a perfect way to worship and serve God. In other words, Messiah would be an even better David and a better Moses all put together.

The problem is that neither David nor Moses perfected the Jews. Not even close! And the *reason* for that is actually quite simple! The ten commandments were written in stone, the books were written on ancient paper, and Kind David ruled extremely well, but like other good kings after him, all their rule was also *external* to the hearts and minds of their subjects just like my Word was external, too, in stone and on paper! In both cases, the Jews had to apply their personal wills to the fullest, meaning all their emotions, all their mind, and strength in seeking and serving me. Service to me involves that strong a commitment of will. But their will was inherently damaged from the time Adam and Eve fell even though I chose the children of Israel and blessed them very deeply. That's why I had to give them services to perform so they could repent and be forgiven when they failed.

Now, there *was* a way for them to actually perfect themselves to the *standard* I gave them. I had given the Jews borders to protect, a country of their own to live in, and I *warned* them not to make allegiance with the other peoples around them. I also told them to drive out particular people because if they disobeyed Me in any of this, the evil people would coerce them to fail. The Jews, as a whole, were very kind-hearted, and they didn't listen on either of these accounts and the rest of their many falls are recorded. Had they listened, they could have dwelt perfectly to the standard I gave them at the time.

And this highlights the problem for Messiah. It would *never* be enough to be the greatest ruler ever, if that ruler remained *external* to the people! The same is true of the greatest spiritual leader, even if they were greater than Moses. But not only this because Messiah had to bring a *better* spirit to the people than what they had of old. So that frames the question: How can Messiah be both King *and* spiritual leader *inside* people *and* give them a *better* spirit than what they were made from, *even* better than the Jews whom I had blessed and nourished their spirits many times over beyond any other peoples?

For you conservative Jews, you make this awkward assumption that *really* is beneath your intelligence. Your great Rabbis whom you follow claim that just the mere *external* presence of Messiah, *only* a man, will be so *very* holy, that he will exude such a spirit. The problem with this? This man you envision is still only made out of the same spirit I made Adam and Eve from, and remember, I made them with the *best* that I had and they fell. Are you Rabbis saying you can best Me? But not only that. Messiah is directly related to giving a *new* heart and spirit to mankind. How could a man even imagine to do so since he didn't even make his *own* soul? And how could a mere man best what I, the Lord, have already done in making Adam and Eve. For that matter, how can *I* even best Myself? So what you try to force in your theology, frankly, doesn't even make sense, *and you know it!* The giver of the *new* heart and new spirit *has to come from* the One who made the first heart and spirit for *all* mankind and who must have real knowledge of *all* mankind.

Now, don't think me ignorant of your theology. You claim Messiah will be a Living Torah. And some of you even go so far as to make *him* in your own studying image, that he will study the *external* Scripture so very deeply that he *becomes* the very Torah. I assure you, *no* man has the ability to become God! Nor does any man have the ability to become *the* Light, for My infinity dwarfs any infinity you could attain, that anyone could obtain. But infinity is why you also fool yourselves because you do in fact sense the infinity *you* could obtain, but you then mistakenly assume it's *My* infinity. To potentially give the new heart and spirit to *all* mankind, *that* can only come from My Infinity which *contains* all of each human being's infinities! Have I now humbled you just a bit?

Let Me explain more deeply. You also know that Torah was, indeed, the very first that God brought forth, and that Torah *is* the plan for *all* Creation through which *all* was created. You *claim*, that this *man only*, would somehow study the Holy Scripture so very deeply, and pray so deeply that he becomes purely Torah. But again, you are still faced with the problem that the Spirit of *that* Torah has *not* gained any spiritual substance to make Him *better* than what he was when he made Adam and Eve perfect! By your *own* descriptions this is true.

In your estimation, Messiah is the Living Torah of *old*, the same that made Adam and Eve who failed. But also, Torah brings forth *all* mankind and so each one would potentially need a new heart and new spirit. There is no mortal consciousness able to reserve that, not even any angel. Remember, every single being I created is unique and though every single being is, in its own right, a potential infinity, that single infinity is only one amongst an infinite number of infinities! Now do you see why no man, nor even angel, can become God or that Light which is Torah? In other words, your conceived mechanism doesn't work! It doesn't bear the test of your *own* scrutiny, if you are not too afraid to think clearly about this. Only omnipresence can contain *all* reality!

And to Christians, I take the opportunity here to remind you that the Lord Jesus Christ said, It is better for you that I go away, for if I go not away, the Comforter, which is the Holy Ghost, even the Spirit of Truth, will not come to you. But if I depart, I will send him unto you, and *He* shall teach you all things, and lead you into all Truth. He will reprove the world of sin, of righteousness, and judgment. Dear Christians, ahh, is this Holy Ghost the Holy Bible made of paper and ink, and external to you? Which is greater, the Holy Ghost *in* you or the Bible *outside* of you? For I told you that I dwell with you, but shall be *in* you.

Fascinating! What you Jews call the *Christian* Messiah, even *he* said it was better that he goes away! Why? Because external rule, which, as I said, his disciples expected from him, wasn't good enough for us! The Messiah requires a *free* way to rule us from within *and* to be recognized as *the* King of Kings *and* to inherit the throne of David which would *then* enable that throne to be brought to where it belonged, in Heaven, *the* Heaven, when Messiah ascends into Heaven to present himself before Almighty God as the *only* acceptable sacrifice to God the Father. Why acceptable? Because through *experiencing* all that evil, and death, itself, within a *mortal* life, Messiah built up new strength and understanding within mortality that didn't exist before, thereby creating the means to best himself, to truly make us a new heart and new spirit. No Rabbi, nor even angel could ever be able to do such a thing with the required effectiveness except *the* Torah from the very beginning.

Instead of you Rabbi's believing that somehow one of you would become so very holy that you actually become *the* Torah, wouldn't it make so much more sense to you that *the* Torah simply came down to *you* in *all* his entirety from conception, to birth, and finally through death? Remember now the requirements to make you a *new* heart and spirit. If, at any time Messiah would fail then he is *not* able to make a *new* heart and spirit for mankind because failing belongs to the old one. In other words, Messiah *must* be perfect throughout his whole mortal lifetime. Dear Rabbi's, you *know* this is true. Better is the man that humbleth himself before the Lord than the man who boasts his own virtue. And if you are going to say that, well, one of us Rabbi's might be born like that, I simply say, yes, it is I! And only *I* can be tempted in *all* ways that every single unique human being can be tempted because *I* make them *all.*

So, conservative Jews, my question to you is this: *The* Torah in Heaven, the one you claim to follow and love with all your heart, soul, mind and strength, are you *blaspheming* in your love for another *besides* Almighty God? How foolish a question? Why? Because Torah is *the* perfect way to love and serve Almighty God. So, in fully honoring Torah, that is the *only* way to fully love and honor Almighty God.

My next question to you is this: Do you think Torah is omnipresent? Omniscient? I think if you consider that *the* Torah we are talking about said in Proverbs chapter 8 that all those that find Me find life and all those that hate me love death, and also, I speak of how I *rejoice* with both God and man, well, I really think you are intelligent enough to see that I, Torah, am *conscious* Spirit, *conscious* Life, *conscious* Love, and not merely paper and ink, and that then, being the closest to Almighty God of all, we would naturally conclude, since Torah *is* the plan for *all* things including all things *conscious,* that

Torah would indeed need a certain level of *conscious* omniscience and omnipresence for I am the chief minister to all. But there is more.

We know Torah comes from the depths, from the very heart of Almighty God, yet we also know Torah loves Almighty God perfectly *and* this is *not* expressed as a *self-love* that Almighty God has for Himself. This is very clearly a *free will* offering of Love for Almighty God as described in Proverbs chapter 8 among many other places in Scripture! Well, how did *that* happen? Let there be Light?

From the Masoretic text in Proverbs 8, The Lord made me as the beginning of his way, the first of his works of old. Doesn't this sound like Torah to you, oh wise ones? I mean, he is *speaking* to us right there. Now, is it *beyond* the love that Torah is, to desire to *give up* my omnipresence so that *my* very perfect will could be *born* into my chosen people? But *not* as a man and woman conceive together, for the iniquity of the fathers passed down to their children was *not* appropriate for such a birth! And unlike a man born into the world, who also has his help-meet born into the world after him, I have no such meager inheritance of unity, but my bride would be all to whom receive My Spirit once I had perfected a *new* heart and a *new* spirit for mankind by *experiencing* that which I had not experienced before.

What had I not *experienced* that was such a necessity? Well, if I, *the* Torah, was going to make mankind a *new* heart, and a *new* spirit, wouldn't it have to be done *from the inside out?* Isn't that the *best* way to do it? From *inside* mortality? I know you know it is. In other words, Torah gives up omnipresence, the truest expression of love and humility, and joins Himself to humanity, but *Being Torah,* also means I am your Lord, it *means* I AM that king, that Messiah prophesied to take the throne of David. But instead of an external, earthly rule, I perfect the new heart and new spirit for you by my last required endurance of suffering through death. Yet, as you read of me, whosoever keeps Torah, shall *not* suffer corruption, and so, like I gave up my omnipresence for love of you and Almighty God, so, too, did I give up my mortality for the same, and Almighty God then glorified me by returning my omnipresence to Me *but* all of my earthly experience remained within me, all of that new strength and new understanding through *experiencing* humanity remained in me. But not only that, but Almighty God deemed me rightfully worthy to ascend back to Heaven from whence I came, and *thus* I correct the children of Israel's great sin in asking for an earthly throne. I brought that throne back to where it belonged but after having come down and joining myself to *you!* An inheritance *indeed!* I Love you.

All this is why I said unto you when I was here that, For the Father judgeth no man, but has committed all judgment unto the Son: That all men should honor the Son, even as they honor the Father. He that honoreth not the Son honoreth not the Father which hath sent him. . . . And hath given him authority to execute judgement also, because he is the Son of man. The living Torah is indeed King in Heaven and on Earth.

Well, being Torah, I already had that authority, didn't I? But how much more perfect my judgement becomes after experiencing *being* human! Right? Is there, or could there be *any* more *perfect* a Messiah than this? You can use your imaginations now, if you want. Try to create in your imaginations something more perfect than what I just described with an actual mechanism that *makes sense!* Go ahead. If you think you have done that, tell me! I'll hear you, and I will answer you! From the inside out I will answer you, because *all* My ways are in understanding. There is *nothing* froward or perverse in them. And I love you, and delight in making you wise. But being My chosen people means you are the children of Humility! As well as Truth, Love, Understanding, Wisdom, Life, Justice, and Peace.

And is there a more perfect rule than allowing *you* the opportunity to freely, *perfectly* serve me by you *choosing* to receive a *new* heart and a *new* spirit that would forever keep you holy, that conquers *all* evil? Is there a more perfect rule than from the *inside out? Your* inside out which keeps you within Love, Life, Wisdom, Justice, Peace, Truth, Understanding being one with the Essence of Reality. A rule for each and every one of you that loves me enough to give up completely your old will to receive the new one that I bought for you with the price of *my* very own mortality.

CHAPTER 11

CHRISTIANITY – WHAT YOU ARE *STILL* MISSING

You saw in the chapter to the conservative Jews, I said it was better for you that I go away! Why better? Because external rule of Goodness wasn't good enough for you! But I pause here to ask you a question I have already asked before, but it bears repeating. Which is greater to you: The Holy Bible or the Lord Jesus Christ while I was here on Earth? The man whose hand I use to write these words has asked that question to many Christians and they *all* have answered that Me being here on Earth is greater, though one actually gave pause to think a while about it. They have rightly determined this. Yet, I said it was better that I go away, because if I go not away, the Holy Ghost will not come to you.

So, do you see that in *My* eyes, for you, the Holy Ghost is better for you than Me just being present on Earth with you? *Why* is the Holy Ghost better? Because when you, *if you,* freely accept it, it guides you *from the inside out* into all truth, but not only that, it brings you the *new* heart, and *new* spirit I made for you! And if I, when present with you on Earth, am better than the Holy Scriptures for you, and if the Holy Ghost is better than I being on Earth for you, *then* the Holy Ghost is *better* for you than the Holy Scriptures! Do you follow the logic?

Why better? Because you are made new from the inside out. Because you have my *Word,* which is true *meaning,* living *inside* you, *not* as a matter of studying paper and ink, but as a matter of My actual *presence* living *inside* of you within that new heart and new spirit! I in you, and you in Me. So, while you may read Scripture and try to draw in My meaning, a better way is the Holy Ghost which you accept which is a *constant* state of meaning in you, meaning you are actually *being* love, love for Me and your neighbor, not *trying* to be love as when you merely read.

Which is better for you: The paper and ink called the Holy Bible, or the Holy Ghost who *knowing* what is in all people's hearts and minds knows *exactly* when and how to speak to *every single soul?* Which is better for you: The actual sun shining *directly* upon your world or the moon merely reflecting its light? Which is better, a lighted object, or its shadow? In all these analogies you rightly discern the answer. So how come you feel this trepidation with the *meaning* of the analogies?

I know you all too well. You don't trust what I just told you because your leaders spend endless hours pounding into your heads and your hearts, shaking the Holy Bible at you telling you that *this* is the Word of God. But . . . doesn't the Scripture tell you that I said my Word is Spirit? In other words, its *Meaning!* But *not* meaning in the sense of a dictionary definition. No. Much, much stronger, much, much deeper. My *Meaning* is an ever-present *Conscious State,* a Holy Presence that addresses *everything* with a *particular* Understanding and Wisdom.

Take, for example, a word you often find in the Holy Bible: Love. Pick *any* verse in the Holy Bible with that printed word in it. Does the dictionary capture any more than a mere glimmer of the meaning that even you, a lowly human, know that love has? How much *more* does *my* Holy Ghost fill out the *meaning* of that word? Because *my* Holy Ghost has been *specifically* improved for your sakes retaining *all* of my experience while I was with you as a mortal man on Earth. How much *more* is the meaning of the word, love, filled out within the new heart and new spirit that I create for you through my Holy Ghost? Can the paper and ink you call the Holy Bible, which *is* My *printed* word, can it do *any* of what I just described above for you? Didn't I command of old not to make any idols, any graven images to worship?

The Jews have a saying which is true: We Jews throughout history, the present, and future, were all present on the day the Lord God spoke to Moses and the congregation from the Holy Mountain of God. And this is true, for all proceeding generations were inside of those Jews waiting to be born. But I say unto you all, that whosoever receives my Holy Ghost, you were present with Me when I came down to Earth for you, when I suffered for you, and rose from the dead for you. In fact, you are present with me now. And My *presence* in you is far better than clinging only to the paper and ink.

Is *any* of *that* what your leaders and teachers tell you? Or do they stand at the pulpit or as leaders in your classes and *stress* that the paper and ink, the Holy Bible *is* the Word of God? What do they tell you about the Holy Ghost? What do they tell you about *how* to receive it, what is *required?* Do they *really* trust Me? Do they trust the Holy Ghost inside or do they *stress* that we must *always* check ourselves against . . . what? Yes, the paper and ink. For whoso strays from trusting the *paper and ink,* well, they risk being excommunicated, right? But how well do *they* trust even the paper and ink? The Holy Bible testifies of *exactly* what I am speaking about to you. You've probably read it many times, but how well do you really understand it? Because they *interpret* those sections to you and *make sure* you have *their* understanding of it, but *not* mine! Do you feel how uncomfortable you are right now reading this? As if I am trying to turn you *against* Me! When I'm trying to turn you more *towards* Me!

You trust the paper and ink because you feel you can easily recognize letters and the words they form. It's *physically* visible to you, and a dictionary can always define a word. But aren't you a people of *My Faith?* Is that faith seen physically? And what is it inside you that *actually* even now gives you faith in Me? Isn't it a deep understanding, a *knowing* of what Goodness is and what it would and will do? You see *that* clearly in your hearts, your minds, your souls, and *no one* taught it to you! And as I call it to your minds and hearts now, you *know* that you have that faith *not* because you read it, or even heard it preached! *Your* faith, *real* faith in Me, is as innate to you as the goodness is that I made you out of! That's how integral a part of you your faith is in Me! Even all these words in this book of *fiction* is not telling you something that isn't already in you at various stages of development! As it is written, My sheep *hear* my voice. Well, *what* is it in you doing the hearing? Something already good and waiting to hear the truth. And once heard, *this* is hearing, indeed.

Now, I'm not going to tell you that your leaders purposefully deceive you, not all of them, but they *are* keenly aware that they need to *control* their flock, and they have a very *sharp* sense of when you, well, sort of begin to lean towards trusting in My Spirit *ahead of* the paper and ink. And if I bring to you an understanding that, while it doesn't disagree with the Holy Bible, it may be hard for these Bible scholars to recognize the truth of it because the *meaning* you speak *isn't the rote word for word Scripture,* well, my goodness, you are using *different* words! How dare you! How *dare you* speak in *meaning!* Doesn't matter if it's *true!* You spoke in *meaning* and not *by the letter.* And herein rests your weakness, oh my dear Christians. And your enemies are fully aware of this which is why them twisting *meaning* works so well on you and especially your children.

Your enemies fight on the *meaning* level but you just repeat quotes like a parrot. That's like bringing a knife to a gunfight. For instance, your enemies tell you that you are *haters* because you don't *love* everyone. Love your enemy. You should *love* the perverse. And since your *mind* is too literal, you say that you *do* love the perverse, just not the sin. But your enemies are sadly wiser than you and call you out on your hypocrisy, saying, You don't *really* love us, cause you don't *accept* us. You shun us, teach against us. But you say that the Bible says marriage is for one man and one woman. And they say how unfair you are to forbid them from loving, for denying them for their whole life loving another human being the way you do. Don't tell us we don't love! And the Bible commands us to *love.*

Now your heart rightly revolts against their meaning but your mind tells you that the Holy Scripture tells you to love them but just hate the sin. Some of you even *think* they can love each other as long as they don't have sex with each other. But your *heart* is correct in denying *all* this because it understands meaning your mind does not! Your heart perceives through feeling that the perverse are not just committing *acts* of sin, but that the perverse dwell in a continual conscious *state* of sin that *exceeds* and is different from just the fallen state of mankind, because they have an *orientation* that *only* produces sin, and that this is *not* acceptable, that the perverse *person* is not acceptable but condemned. Even that this perverse person should *not* be loved! That they are different from sinners who do wrong but have the capacity to stop *being* that sin after it is done. Even an adulterer or a murderer in the very moment after they have sinned, can turn away from it. Those sins are not produced by a conscious state of that sin, not produced from an orientation to *be continually* that sin. Do you see the difference now between a rote approach and *meaning?* Do you see now why I burned up Sodom and Gomorrah? Remember the holy printed words from Noah's time that every imagination of the thoughts of their hearts were only evil continually? Now does your mind understand?

Is the Holy Scripture given to you to memorize letters or is it given to you for *meaning?* But who wrote the Bible, your enemies quip. Which translation, how *many* translations, go dig *deep* in the earth and find some ancient stone with very weathered letters you don't recognize and see if you can make things even clearer! And *then,* of course they clearly point out to you your leader's hypocrisies, their failings, and then they also make their *own* interpretations of the same letters you use. But then again, you have *differences* between your different Christian faiths, too. But, is my *meaning* dependent upon all those things or is my true meaning accessible to every individual if they just seek me?

When I was here on Earth, did I *ever* act as if I *needed* the Holy Scriptures to justify *Me?* True, I quoted them a few times, but in a greater context of My *Meaning* for your sakes? I merely showed you we are in agreement.

Do you know how much more power there is in *knowing* true *Meaning?* What do you think the Holy Ghost does, quote Scriptures to you all day long? Oh, it does make reference to them from time to time *after* the Holy Ghost teaches you the true meaning of something! *Then* it shows you the printed word that refers to that meaning and often a holy person will say, Wow, I've read that so many times but I *never* saw *that* beautiful meaning before.

And how does a *holy* person know they have the true meaning? Well, you see, that question is just what your ignorant leaders drive into your hearts and *somehow* they think by hammering in the paper and ink, the *letters* of the Holy Scripture, that *this* will somehow protect you against . . . what? True *meaning?* Because you sure fight against it! They think a holy person knows true meaning by memorizing the Holy Bible! Polly Parrot want a cracker?

But *how* does a holy person know they have the true meaning? *I AM! All* of My meaning has that quality about it. The *meaning* is self-revealing, self-supporting in Goodness, unchallengeable in Understanding and Wisdom and the other five of My Spirits which you receive with the Holy Ghost. Unchallengeable except by those who love the external paper and ink and the control they think they have through it? *Where does it say that in the Holy Scriptures,* they always ask. So weak it grieves me. Do you not perceive how much more powerful the *meaning* of Goodness is? And that even the printed Word has its power from the true *meaning* that is there *if* you haven't utterly destroyed it through your laborious control and repetition! Are you now seriously asking, what *is* meaning?

Every soul is unique, in a different condition of *meaning,* at a unique time and place with it and My Holy Ghost knows when and how to speak to anyone the *meaning* that will touch them. The Holy Scriptures have no such knowledge. They don't know *anything*. They are paper and ink. My Word is *true meaning,* and from thence is Light. The paper and ink is like a *shadow* of My meaning, and many people draw within that shadow what they *think* it means.

Here is another question: For what leader did I die to give you? Not *even* for the disciples, your Popes, but for *only* one leader. The Holy Ghost. There is no better leader, and *never* will be. Do your leaders and teachers act like that? Do they inspire *that* particular knowledge and faith within you? Or do they tell you that you *can't* trust what's inside you, let alone anything you *think* you perceive that *might* be the Spirit of God. But the paper and ink, now *that's* something you know you can trust.

Some of your leaders, if they are reading this, will immediately accuse the man whose hand is recording this, of saying that *he's* saying you can't trust the Bible, you can't trust the Word of God. Please look more closely then at what is *written* here. No where do I say that, nor even *imply* that. But what I *have* given you is the truth about what the printed word is and what it is not, what it can do and what it *can't* do.

Now, I hope you are able to receive what I tell you next. It won't be easy for you, but it is *True*, and quite necessary for you to understand. There is something *all* Christian religions have in common and it *is* the cause of a common weakness in you which, again, your enemies exploit. Satan makes sure they will exploit it, he teaches them how! So really, your enemies are being guided by *their* spirit. Are you being guided by yours? If they are guided by spirit and you are *not,* then you are at a great disadvantage! But *this* isn't what I mean to speak to you about. This just sets the stage.

A common tenet within *all* Christianity is the following: We are all sinners and need to repent. No one is perfect except the Lord Jesus Christ. No one is perfect except God. You *cannot* be perfect. Now, some Christian leaders add to this that if you claim to be perfect then you are a *terrible* sinner worthy to be cast out if you continue in your delusion. This is really, basically the same belief the Pharisees had about me. Now, the Christians teach the same about *My* holy children!

Let's start with the first part: We are all sinners and need to repent. Do you say this *only* of people *before* they repent and are saved? Or does this also include everyone *after* they repent and are 'saved'? You say it, you *teach* it about *all* of them, before *and* after. Now your enemies rightfully mock you on this because even though they don't believe in Me, they understand enough about Me to know that *you* are mocking *Me* by holding that ridiculous belief! They ask, What *kind* of salvation is it? Wait a minute. You are *still* sinners like us, still have the *same* evil hearts like us, for even your Bible says sin proceedeth from the heart, and yet you say you are *saved?* Saved from *what?* Not from sinning. Not from an evil heart. Then *what?*

And to this you respond: We are saved by grace from hell, because we *believe* that the Lord Jesus Christ died for us. And they rightfully mock you in this even further. You mean all Jesus did with *all* that he did was just give you a *belief?* And this seems absurd to them, and it is! Because deep inside these *non-believers* they feel that if Jesus is *indeed* the Son of God, the co-Creator, then he could do *better* than that. *And I did!* In fact, Christians false dogma cause many to blaspheme me, and maybe, just maybe, if they hear the real Truth about Me, they would actually come to truly be saved!

Dear Christians, do you really think that I would allow Satan's boast that as long as you are mortal you *have to* bow to Satan? That I *cannot* make you holy in your mortal lifetime? So Satan can outdo me in that my loyal followers will have to bow to him and sin, too? Does this sound right to you?

Are you now reaching into the dogma your leaders have falsely taught you and *that* dogma now conflicts in your hearts with the questions you just answered *rightly* about me! Who are you going to believe? Your faith that tells you that, indeed, I *can* make you perfect even in this mortal life, or the dogma which is *worthy* to be mocked because it is *that* ridiculous! Plainly put, if it was only a *belief* that I needed to generate in you, I would not have had to suffer like I did for you. There were far easier ways to get you to *believe*. But only *One Way* to make a new heart and new spirit for you! How could it be new if it's still sinning like the old?

Which is the preferred grace? Claiming you are sinners like everyone else but *you* get to go to Heaven because you *believe,* or, I give you a new heart and a new spirit that purifies you of all ungodliness so that there remains in you nothing that will cause you to sin? Which of these two feels like what I would do? What I *could* do? Which of these two matches what I went through for you, overcoming all evil *in the flesh* including death, itself? Which of these two matches the law of old?

Here's a question: If someone smacks you on your right cheek then turns and says forgive me, and then you do, but then he turns and smacks you with his other hand on the left cheek. Is he still forgiven because he asked before? Was his repentance the first time sincere? Was the flaw that caused him to sin the first time *still* there at the second time? What is required for *true* repentance? If you find the way to give *all* of yourself to Me, your *whole entire* will and allow Me to come into you and make you new, then is there something I will leave undone? *Still* corrupt? And remember what I am using to make you that new heart and new spirit. I am using Myself, who was mortal, who became human, and sinned not, who overcame even death through leading the perfect *mortal* holy life. Truly, I AM the Way, the Truth, and the Life and able to give you . . . what? The same!

Now some of you might be saying within yourselves about yourselves, "I don't have what you describe. I didn't think that was possible." Well, weren't you taught that it *isn't* possible? Can you receive what you *don't* believe? You see, your belief *can't* save you. No *belief* has power to save. But *not* believing does block what you don't believe I could do for you. Consider this: You love me so dearly and you open fully to Me, you ask me to forgive you for *everything*, and so I *begin* to forgive you by drawing closer to you. You've told me how wretched you are, what you've done, that you are worthy to *die*, but now I draw closer to you, to the goodness you are made out of that is crying to me to save you from such a horrible, shameful state. And so my Perfect Holy Presence draws closer and closer to you to rid you of your weakness, your ignorance, your ungodliness, and to make you new, to make you perfect! Because in truth, *you asked me to make you PERFECT.* And yes, I meant to shout that at you!

But as I draw closer to you with my Perfection, my Holiness, there is yet something of your old self you are still holding on to. You asked for me to take all of you, *but*, as my Presence draws closer to you, as my Light shines on you more brightly, you see something in you, *feel* something in you that you hadn't felt before. You are not worthy to be in the presence of my Light.

Right *there! THERE!* What do you do next? If you decide to then *not* go back on your word, and to take hold of this newly discovered corruption and give *that* back to me as well, and *then* leave yourself *completely* open to me to enter fully into you, and not only that, when I draw even *closer*, you embrace me with all you have, then in that embracing, in *only* wanting My Spirit, that completes within you the full process of completely repenting, completely turning again to me and fully loving me, and *that* action allows me to do *only* my Will in you!

You didn't just come to Me to let go, to repent, to be rid of your guilt, you *also* came to me to be made whole, to be made holy! And to do *that*, you have to fully embrace *I AM*. When you see through your spirit My Presence near you and you feel me there, or for some of you, you will see in a vision that I am there, then it makes perfect sense to you to open your hearts to fully embrace such goodness.

Now let's back up a bit. But as I draw closer to you with my Perfection, my Holiness, there is yet something of your old self you are still holding on to. You asked for me to take all of you, *but,* as my Presence draws closer to you, as my Light shines on you more brightly, you see something in you, *feel* something in you that you hadn't felt before. You are not worthy to be in the presence of my Light. Right *there!* THERE! What do you do next? And you say in your hearts, "I can't be perfect! No one can be perfect. I can't take the Lord's perfection so close to me. I am not worthy!"

I, the Lord, even I can't force you. Love never forces. You are free. And though I have love for you, you won't allow me to freely love you the *only* Way I know how! And you haven't loved Me fully the way that *part of you knows how!* Because that *damned* lie stops you! You have believed the lie more so than the goodness you are made out of telling you not to believe that lie. What can I do?

No one can be perfect but God? Aren't two-thirds of the angels perfect? Those Heavenly angels *are* and always have been perfect and holy! They are not Me. They are not Almighty God. And I made *you* to eventually become *even* higher than they! *Not* because, as some of you foolishly believe, the angels have no free will. Thy will be done on Earth as it is on done Heaven. That's not Me *forcing* you or transforming you to *not* have free will! My will be done *freely* on Earth as it is done *freely* in Heaven! Now do you understand? Gave I this prayer for your sakes to mean *on the other side of life* after *I return,* or for your mortal lifetimes?

Consider this: Take a three-year-old little child and teach them that God is all Good and wants us to be good. The devil is bad, and wants us to do bad things. Now ask the child, which one says this: You cannot be perfect, you *have to* do wrong, *be* wrong. What will that child tell you? How come that child knows better than you?

There are many other possible reactions you might have. I simply cannot write in this *fiction* all of them, but I do want to mention one more. Suppose you *do* receive my Holy Ghost as is *natural* for the goodness you are made out of to do, and you do so without question *but then*, after you are holy, Satan comes to you and says, You *know*, no one is perfect. You *can't* be *perfect*. Then what do you do? The Holy Ghost inside you is showing you that, indeed, it is perfect, and that, indeed, it is *inside* you, but also you are *inside* Him! But Satan keeps at you. He *hates* to lose a soul. He points out how utterly *ignorant* you are. You don't *know* everything.

Oh, the devil is so tricky, and none more clever than when he is actually *telling you the truth!* But for a corrupt purpose and with a subtle lie intertwined. Human perfection does *not* entail being omniscient! Only God is omniscient. Human perfection isn't *all* of what God's perfection is!

Then Satan will catch you in desire *after* you are holy. Oh, he says, *look* at you, you are *sinful*. You *lust*. Now here is where ignorance can kill you. What's the difference between the natural God-given desires and lust? I made you with a body of flesh but also with a human heart, even the new one. And even your soul has natural desires. There is *nothing* sinful in the *natural* desires of goodness. But as mentioned before about King David, there is a right way, and a wrong way to go about it. What is it about adultery and fornication that so displeases me?

Those two sins aren't the same, either! Adultery isn't just sin with another person, it's sin against the spouse of that person as well, and against their whole household. And the consequences are far more destructive than fornication limited between just the intimate partners. Adultery also breaks an oath and trust between family members that *had* been based on goodness. Yet, there is also something both sins have in common.

You call it making love. But what do you call it when you love the body more than the person inside? Isn't that the case with both fornication and adultery? Because you fulfil the physical act of 'love' in its entirety, and some of you go to great lengths with this, but do you honor the person inside that body with the same fervor? Why not? Because you *really* don't want to be *that* engaged with that person, or, if you are already married, then you *can't* fully fulfill obligations to that person. Either way, you have *reversed* the order of Creation! I made the body for the sake of the person inside, but through fornication and adultery, you have, at best, *put up with* the person for the sake of their body, or, sorry, but I simply *can't* honor your person as much as your body because I'm *married* to another. I don't like when My Creation is turned inside-out, upside-down, backwards, or generally perverted because all this comes with great destruction and offence to goodness. Be that as it may, your *desire* is natural. It's the follow-through that will kill you.

So Satan says to you, Aha, what *kind* of holiness? You just lusted after that one *right there!* And you *did* have a desire flash in an instant, mostly brought on by the other person *calling it forth from you!* But it's really a mutual thing. That's how life works. But what does the *person* you are do with it? If you get deep enough within the Holy Ghost, you can be sped up sufficiently to actually see the call of desire approach you, instead of it being so instantaneous. That gives you time to completely interrupt its effect before it happens, if you so desire! Or you may feel the desire is appropriate so you investigate who this *person* is. Proceed with true love, respect, and integrity and there is no sin there in your desires.

But Satan wants to set up the impossible for you so that he can then tell you that you *failed*. You should *never* have desired! And what happens to you if you believe that lie? Well, then you believe he has power of you. And even though he didn't, he does once you believe the lie! And *then* he can bring another temptation against you, and you will fall because you *falsely* believed you had to! You see, Satan's whole game is getting you to believe a lie, *any* lie, because then he can play off that and convince you that you can't help failing and *then* he'll make things so hard on you that when he tempts you, you don't believe you can resist. Or, what's the point of resisting when I'm going to fail anyway! Oh, he has many variations of his tricks and he keeps trying different ones till one works!

Satan knows *exactly* what will cause you pain, what will wear you down. If he convinces you of a lie, that undermines your strength. Well, *remember*, you've already lusted for her, just imagine now how good it would be. It's only imagination. *There* she is. Go say Hi! It's just a hello. Then when your desire comes again, it's quite a bit stronger. After all, you've been imagining this. And *now* she's interacting with you more and feeding your feelings. And Satan says, look at what your feeling *now!* It's really irresistible. You may say, no, it is resistible, but then Satan just keeps playing the same game over and over again until your desire overpowers you and *then* you really do lust, the commitment to desire *regardless* of the person inside!

Now let's back up a bit. So Satan says to you, Aha, what *kind* of holiness? You just lusted after that one *right there!* And your response is, No I didn't. Attracted for sure, but what kind of love, what kind of life if I don't look beyond this? Then you seek more knowledge of the person, and if you find the person isn't right for you, your desire slips away. If you feel the person *is* right for you, then your desire grows. And that is perfectly fine. It's *not* lust.

But what to do if you haven't thought any of this through *beforehand*. Those who spend a good amount of time seeking me, seeking *how* to receive the Holy Ghost, they rise and fall many times, but each time they rise with more strength, more understanding. By the time they *do* become holy, they've had quite a good bit of training against Satan's tricks and lies. They've also gotten used to seeking me deeply and calling out to me for the goodness that beats the evil that is trying to destroy them.

But if you are able to receive the Holy Ghost more easily, and some do, some *are* able, well, you're going to have to fight those same battles on the *other side* of salvation, and *that* means, you are *now* holy, don't mess it up, learn how to keep it. And as I said, the Holy Ghost will teach you all things and lead you into all truth.

This is so *very* different from the way Christians approach serving God and putting all their trust in the paper and ink, instead of my Holy Spirit. Only My Spirit can help you win. Only my Holy Ghost can speed you up faster than temptations can swallow you up. Only my Holy Ghost can give you time to step aside and let the temptations pass on by. Only my Holy Ghost can prove to you that your desire isn't lust when it isn't and when Satan is telling you it is. Only my Holy Ghost can untangle the webs of deceit that get woven around you. Because I AM a conscious presence within your thoughts and emotions and you are within Me. So when Satan tries to reorientate you to his perspective, you instantly feel it's foreign and reject it because you identify with me and My goodness as being you, not what Satan claims to be you.

When you first realize the Lord Jesus Christ *is* the Son of God and fully worthy to be worshipped and sought for salvation, My Holy Spirit immediately comes to dwell *with* you. I may even make some internal changes in you as you have requested. It is *right there* where your leaders and many of you make the mistake in thinking you just attained salvation, when all you have done is just begun! Or, your leaders tell you that you have to add a certain *ritual* first and *then* you are saved. But if you keep seeking Me, seeking to gain more and more of my Holy Presence, seeking more Understanding, I will teach you in Spirit.

And one of the first things I show you is *you!* Like you have never seen nor understood yourself before. You *need* that if you are to effectively gather yourself up and fully offer yourself to Me. Without *that,* the things you don't understand about your own self will be used against you to drag you down. And it is also within those things that you *still* hold on to your old will and prevent me from giving you a new one with a new heart and new spirit. Or, if you receive the Holy Ghost and *then* you become aware of things about yourself that you didn't know before, and all of you will because my Light shows you like never before, then the Holy Ghost engages you in a process that reorientates you concerning those very things, that puts them all within your new, holy perspective and they fall away from you like the husk of a seed when it sprouts. By the way, this is not as easy as it sounds, but fully within your new abilities. Just don't think that *after* you become holy, you get to put your feet up! You'll have to pursue me with even more fervor! Because you have been blessed with so much more potential and strength and all.

Many people believe they *have* offered themselves fully, at least that's how it *feels* to them, but sadly, they have not, or, I know it's better for them to wait longer to fully receive Me. Either way, My Spirit will come to show them what they need to do next. Sadly, if they believe they have already been 'saved,' well, they may take my next advice or not, because, after all, 'I'm *saved,*' they say to themselves, and then, 'But of course I'll still sin, everybody *knows* that's the way it works.' And after a while, they pay less and less attention to My Spirit trying to get them to see the Truth, and reading my word just becomes more and more rote. After a while, leaders who have fallen into this trap even teach others just to repeat the prayer whether you feel it or not, understand it or not, even in a language you don't understand. They say I will hear that noise and bless you, anyway. Very sad indeed.

That process in you of believing you are *saved,* when you are not, and then you know you have to sin *anyway,* that kind of process hollows you out. That is the reason all of your Christian religions are failing and why the youth turn away from you, because while it takes you so very long to see this problem, the youth see it very quickly and then toss Me aside along with your wretchedness. It's a terrible mistake which in the end makes the younger generation *worse* than you!

Now I would like you to consider this: 'If you *were* to realize you are *not* 'saved' yet, but you *definitely* do have love for Me, what harm would it do to you and others if you simply told the truth like this: You know, I love the Lord so much, but I don't feel I'm saved yet. You know, I think I would know that better than anyone else! But I am going to keep seeking the Lord with all my heart, all my mind, all my soul, and strength until I really receive the Holy Ghost and *am* saved.

Then other Christians will come to you, quote the Holy Scripture to you, and then say, No, no, you are *already* saved. See, it says so right here in the Bible. Now you might be disturbed by that because they know the Bible much better than you. Well, Satan knows every word in there, too! And how to twist it up. Please don't be troubled. Ask of Me, and ye shall receive. I'll have you open the Bible up in your own privacy just between you and Me, and I'll show you the true meaning, where they told you wrong, and *why* it's wrong, and *why* what I show you is right!

Do you know what that *why* is? It's *meaning!* Something the Christians are mostly short on! I'll teach you in the privacy of your own heart, mind, and soul true *meaning* that they don't have, that they have *never* even thought about. And when you see them again and they ask you if you have finally come to the Light, you can tell them with confidence, "Actually, I *have,* and let me tell you what the Lord has shown me and *why* I am not yet saved, but He is gracious to those who wait on Him in spirit and in Truth!" It may be that you will *actually* convince some of them, or even all of them. The days of persecution are at hand, and they are going to suffer greatly and they are going to feel the lacking of Me with them. It may very well be that they will hear my Truth through you and in time to prepare them. Time. Something that is fast running out for the world you live in.

What happens if you don't receive the Holy Ghost by the time your time runs out here on Earth? You've been seeking all that time really sincerely, and you have been fully honest, but you *know* you haven't made it yet. Something you don't understand still stands in your way. Well, I can tell you of a surety, you will see! What does that mean? You know what it *means.* Just stay on the path you have been walking, even with your last breath. Sometimes it actually takes that long! But isn't it worth it?

Dear Christians, I love you dearly. It's not a small thing that you believe in Me, that you treasure the Holy Bible, my true *printed* word.

Your faith isn't un-noticed by Me, either. But as you know, I cannot change the Truth for anyone, no matter how much I love them. Please heed the meaning delivered to you here in this work of *fiction*.

CHAPTER 12

WHAT MAJOR RELIGION, THE *ONLY* ONE, WAS BORN FROM ...?

Reading the title of this chapter many of you might be instantly conflicted, thinking, Well, that's a *hard* statement to make, or *even,* Who are *you* to judge? Besides the fact the I AM Justice, and Truth, how about I just lay out the facts for you to see for yourself? But before I do this, I want to make clear what happens through generations of telling the same lies.

Whether it be Jewish orthodoxy and misunderstanding Messiah, or Christian common doctrine that misunderstands salvation and the Holy Ghost, or Islam handing down their doctrine for a mere millennium plus a few hundred years, the authors of those lies have long been gone, dead and buried, but their *motivations* unfortunately live on within their bequeathed deceit. In each case, *geniuses* – yes, even way back then we had the same kind of arrogant *geniuses* as we have today, people who feel they know better than anyone else and given the opportunity to affect the *masses,* they will do so happily, smiling at the legacy they leave behind for generations to come – decided to be judge over the *ignorant* man and devised doctrines to lock the masses out from the Truth that they felt endangered the *genius's* vison of reality!

In the case of ancient Judaism, they couldn't have *Me* ruin their vision of a Jewish Empire, a Jewish *religion* that *they* authored, and in the case of Christianity, well, once they established a Christian *leadership,* well, *of course* their leadership needed to be protected at all costs, which, by the way, precluded the Holy Ghost from being *anyone's* leader except for those they *officially* deemed as having My Spirit! In both of these cases, *geniuses* had to deal with the *problem* of My Truth already being written down rather plainly, and the fact that they still needed the *authority* that came from those Holy Scriptures. That meant their deception had to find a way to successfully *interpret* the Scriptures to the *ignorant* masses. But for *Islam,* well, its author took a bold new approach – they simply decided to change history all together, to rewrite it, which such effort should make any devout communist feel proud. Both Islam and later communism came up with a totally new *doctrine* to explain mankind, Me, and humanity, as well as history.

The *effect* of creating these lies and wrapping them in a glorious coat of authority and reverence, ensured they would be passed down from generation to generation. But what actually *happens* as these lies are past down? The initial generation of leaders knew *very well* their intended purpose but they *did not* pass *that* knowledge on to their acolytes. Which meant that when leaders were chosen from among them, they didn't know either! This also was intended by the original authors – the later generations' ignorance would serve to add validity and honesty to the doctrine. They felt that ignorance bred innocence, and innocence would be very convincing. And, of course, they told their followers, "Don't question *anything*. That's *blasphemy,* worthy of death." As for Me, I love sincere questions.

So, the generations that followed did *not* have the deceit in their hearts and minds that those *geniuses* had. Nevertheless, they inherited doctrine that is in many ways, but not all, incongruent with Me and My Ways. But, *ahh,* those geniuses *knew* this would be a troublesome development so they also created doctrine to *explain away* those *minor* discrepancies. In fact, they were *so* good at it, that it takes someone like *ME* to untangle it.

When I came to Earth in the flesh, I untangled the lies during that time, but do you really think those *geniuses* were going to stop? No, they just got even better at lying and manipulating people. The point is, all the *followers* today are ignorant and in some ways *innocent* of the deceit of their religious founders. Nevertheless, all that *innocent* corruption that was woven into their false doctrine seriously troubles every single living soul that follows it! No matter how the founders and succeeding *geniuses* have explained it all away, told you to just put up with it, it troubles you. It disturbs the very foundations of your souls because it doesn't align with the Essence of Reality, My Truth, My Understanding, and My Love, My Justice, My Peace, My Wisdom, and My Life.

So they tell you to just have *blind* faith. I *hate* blind faith. It's an oxymoron. True faith in Me comes from knowing, experiencing I AM. From thence is Understanding, knowledge, sight but *never* blindness. Don't you *know* My Word is true? Don't you *know* this book, God's Creative Writing, isn't *fiction?* Paul, in Hebrews chapter 11, seemingly muddied the waters a bit when he connected faith to things hoped for in the future and so not seen yet, *however,* he *never* based his current actions and state upon a whimsical hope for the future but upon his *present* faith coming from *present knowledge and sight* from the Holy Ghost within him. He testified to that all the time but proponents of *blind* faith love to misquote his *meaning*.

And so now, let Me deal with *Islam*. Please, you followers of the Koran, keep in mind and heart what I just explained about you, and harden not your hearts like your founders did towards Me. The Koran was designed to make you feel good about yourselves, important no matter your lot in life, no matter your poverty or your suffering, *even if you kill yourselves in its service!* And when I say, kill yourselves, I don't mean it in any respectable sense of glorious martyrdom. I mean it as the most egregious unforgivable sin against me.

Let Me start off explaining to you why suicide is unforgivable. In order to be forgiven, you have to be so while you are *yet* mortal, because forgiveness requires true repentance, and repentance requires you turn yourselves completely away from all sin and give yourselves completely up to Me, asking me to turn you fully towards Me. When done right, I give you that new heart and new spirit that I died to make for you. You hand over fully to me all of your mortal life and I make you holy, yet within a mortal body. Now *that* takes ultimate courage, being willing to be holy, mortal, and constantly in direct conflict with the whole world. *That* is truly giving yourself fully to Me, dying to the world, if you will understand this.

But what happens when you *kill* yourself? Suicide. Your very last decision is self-destruction. There is *no* mortal decision after that one. And your last decision is an absolute affront to the Essence of Reality I just reminded you of a few paragraphs ago. From the very beginning of this work of *fiction*, I explained to you that within my Father Almighty God, and Me, and the Holy Ghost, there is *no* self-destruction. Self-destruction is the epitome of evil and mutually exclusive to GOODNESS, Goodness, and even goodness down to the very insects I created!

At this point, some of you are trying to gather reasons and defenses, saying it's not self-destruction if you are honoring God by killing yourselves because in doing My will, your soul is not going to die. But then, you have to realize that *within* your mortal life, for that reasoning to work, I would *still* have to approve of self-destruction within Me, within life, and as I pointed out, that doesn't exist in Me, not even in an *insect,* not even in a *pig* or a *dog,* which you loathe.

You can also think about it like this: What kind of *weak* God do they serve, who can't give them a way to prevail in serving me *other than* self-destruction? Other than committing an unforgivable act. And the glory for such an act? Most of the time it's not even killing the enemy on the battlefield, it's killing innocent people whom you *don't even know,* but whom *you* judge as evil. But even when I destroyed Sodom and Gomora, I went down *in person* to see had they done altogether according to the cry of their wickedness. But you have no such abilities to perceive the depths of souls. My, my, how *effective* your founder's deception and lies have become, that you think you can honor Me by committing the greatest evils possible! Every fiber of your being pleads with you *not* to commit such abomination but the lies of the doctrine overcome what even the most simple of life forms understand is something that should *not* be overruled by *anything.*

But didn't *I* kill Myself when I was here, you might ask? No. I was crucified. I didn't kill Myself. And had mankind decided *not* to do such a thing to Me, then I would still be with you to this day! Right here on Earth! I was given to be a *man* on Earth, and even when I was tempted in the desert, I did not resort to the heavenly powers I had access to through faith. Because I was upon Earth *not* to save through grand *external* acts of Godly power as Moses performed for the masses, but to make a new heart and new sprit for you to save you through an *internal* act of pure grace for every individual, one at a time! And it was the act of *experiencing* mortal death that allowed me to finish Creating that new heart and new spirit for you! Please stop your foolishness! Yet, the above description doesn't address fully the heart of Islam. Let's examine what the Founder of your *religion* told you.

What was the motivation? The original inhabitants were *pagans.* Pagans surrounded by Jews who had supplanted them many a time. After *that,* the Christians came with *their* religion and supplanted them *again*. All these little tribes of people being *pushed around, bullied* by foreigners with a claim of serving *their* God. It's not hard to understand the resentment you had.

And what was *central* to both invading forces? The Jews claimed *God* gave them their land! A God that organized no less than *twelve* tribes into a cohesive fighting force. And the Christians? Even more impressive, because they came from many different peoples and lands, a religion that easily crossed borders and changed social fabrics. They came holding their crosses up high, they came telling *everyone* that Jesus was the Lord of all, and that He gave them the right to, well, rule over you and oppress you but did *nothing* to improve our lot in life. Why should we always have *foreign* rulers?

So Mohamed, being the *genius* he was, realized the *power* in having a centralizing force for the people, and there was no other centralizing force greater than having a common God to serve. And wouldn't it be nice if *his* people had *their own* God? The problem is, creating such a God out of rock and stone wouldn't match up well against the Jewish or the Christian God. No. And to simply *create* a God out of *thin air,* well, that wouldn't work, either. No.

Mohamed's people needed a God most believable, a God with respectability that could rival the Jews and the Christians! No small feat. Mohamed was indeed *very* intelligent. He knew there could *not* be a God to rival his enemies Gods because their doctrine was too well set, and there was very solid real understanding within it, able to control the masses, and even able to justify the debauchery committed against his people! No. There could never arise a *different* God to challenge that.

So Mohamed studied his enemies quite thoroughly. The secret rested with Jewish history. *Change* that history and you also affect Christianity! Aha! Ishmael was blessed by the Jewish God! Well, what do you know? Mohamed thought to himself, *I* am a descendent of Ishmael! I feel it in my bones. And, well, everyone knows the Jews didn't live up to their God's blessings . . . so, it only makes sense that God would turn to *Ishmael,* to *his* descendants to re-establish a covenant with a blessed people. *We* are the *true* Heirs of *Almighty God,* Mohamed proclaimed inside himself and laughed. The Jews don't have that God anymore, and the Christians, well, just like the Jews say, they are only worshipping a *man,* not Almighty God!

The more Mohamed examined his creation, the more he fell in love with it, because he knew the hatred his people had for the Jews and the Christians, he knew how envious and jealous they were of the power they wielded over them and around the world. But to have our *own* God, a *truly believable* God that would *justify* Mohamed's people and *Mohamed's* followers, well, this had the power to lift these people out of the swamps and poor conditions they lived in, this had a worthy power to assert over all. But then Mohamed returned to the problems of doctrine.

The Jews and the Christians were thick with it. And to outdo *them*, to make *his* God *better* than theirs, well, we'll pray SIX times a day, not just three, and many other rules did Mohamed create to *outperform* the Jews and the Christians. To be holier than them. The problem with this is that ritual does not have the power to save, and, in fact, *excessive* ritual has a converse effect on souls seeking salvation like being stuck in a rut that you just dig deeper and deeper and... But I have to say this, Islam does rival Catholicism for ritual. But there is also a sort of comfort generated by ritual through a false sense of control. Ahhh, *there it is!* Who wouldn't trust the sense of control they get from good ritual? And the more excessive, the *more* control. How opposite this is to my Holy Spirit! I AM doesn't need repetition. In fact, every day is new.

Yes, they needed their *own* believable doctrine. But unlike Christianity, this doctrine had to support *conquering* her enemies. You see, even though Rome had become Christian, that really made little difference to them being *conquerors*, rulers over them, and Mohamed knew Christian doctrine did *not* support it. And the Jews conquering only pertained to *their* land, but Mohamed knew he needed a doctrine, a God, that would send him to conquer the whole world! Because the Christians needed to be defeated all across the world. And he could use the many discrepancies in Christianity to undermine them, even their warlike actions. *But* his *new* religion would not have that hypocrisy. His would indeed be a religion well deserved for *war*. After all, haven't his people been abused long enough? Vengeance makes perfect sense, but *not* a personal vengeance. No, nothing so vein. This had to be a *righteous*, a *holy* vengeance given by the *True God*.

And so Mohamed had a vision! A vision that basically accomplished all that! However, though Mohamed was a true *genius,* yet, he still had the same *heart* of his ancestors who were jealous of my Chosen People, the Jews from ancient times. That *same* heart that I prophesied against through Ezekiel, my Holy Prophet saying: Because you have had a perpetual hatred, and hast shed the blood of the children of Israel by the force of the sword in the time of their calamity, in the time that their iniquity had an end: Therefore, as I live, sayeth the Lord God, I will prepare thee unto blood, and blood shall peruse thee; sith thou hast not hated blood, even blood shall pursue thee. . and I will fill his mountains with his slain men, in thy hills, and in thy valleys, and in all thy rivers . . . I will make thee perpetual desolations, and thy cities shall not return: *AND YE SHALL KINOW THAT I AM THE LORD.*

Therefore, as I live, saith the Lord God, I will even do according to thine anger, and according to thine envy which thou hast used out of thy hatred against them; and I will make myself known among them, when I have judged thee. . . Thus with your mouth ye have boasted against me, and have multiplied your words against me: I have heard them. Ezekiel Ch. 35

Yes, dear Muslims, I have heard your words, so this I ask of you: Does your religion make sense to what you really know of what Goodness is? Love? Truth? Peace? Justice? Wisdom? Understanding? Life? Think for *yourselves.* Seek those seven that I AM and the Truth *will be* revealed to you, because even for you, I have no pleasure in the death of the wicked, but that the wicked repent and live.

No ritual, nothing imposed from the outside-in by you can save you, but My presence from the inside then outward is salvation. Love your enemies isn't an imposed command, because no imposition can truly generate *that* condition. Love that is forced isn't love. It *is* my presence inside a soul that loves and judges truly. And when I send those two special souls to the Earth to pour out my judgements, they won't wield the power of manmade weapons, but My power as Moses and Elijah had been given. They shall truly judge you with My judgement and ye shall know that I AM God. And by the way, they don't kill themselves in a false attempt at foolish glory. After they are done prophesying, I allow *you* to kill *them!* To allow you your sense of power, of victory. But then, after three days I raise them from dead before your very eyes. Do you see the Truth in this? The Love? The Justice? You *will* see it!

As you have read this work of *fiction*, you see I have told you the Truth about all, without holding back. I cannot support anyone or anything except it be born of the Holy Seven that I AM. Think your religion through. Uncover the hostility within it to My Seven, and have true faith in ME. I, indeed, became a man as I explained to you, but before even the first man was, I AM.

And I *never* go back on my Word. I blessed Ishmael to prosper in the Earth, but I blessed Isaac for *eternal* prosperity in heart, soul, mind, body, and spirit! I blessed Jacob, *not* Esau, even though Jacob sinned against me, but as I said, he repented for the rest of his life. And I AM a forgiving God. The Jews *are* My Chosen People, both in *blessing*, but also in *cursing*, because only to *them* as a *nation*, did I call *that* nation to be Holy unto Me. And through *them*, have *all* nations been blessed. Do you *really* have a problem with *that*? Go ahead, let Me know, and as I just recorded unto you from the ancient prophet that described the hearts of your ancestors, *as well as you hearts today*, I give you my Word *again*, I will answer you!

Think about what I AM. Think about what I did, what my Love did for mankind and *why*. It's the why that is crucial to all. No religion

WHAT MAJOR RELIGION WAS BORN FROM ...?

has good answers to why questions, but I do. So seek Me, and I *will* answer you. Go ahead. *Ask Me about your religion, whether it be true or not.* I will come to you and show you plainly where and *why* it is not. I am *not* asking you to ask anyone else about your religion. I am asking you, from the deep goodness that I made you out of, to pray to Me, the God who *is* Goodness, and *ask* for Understanding. If you *don't*, well, that is your choice, and I will respect that according to Justice. You do want Justice, don't you?

One last thing to think about. In the New testament it is recorded *clearly* that I made a promise to mankind that I would not leave them Comfortless, that I would come to them, give them a new heart and new spirit, and that the Holy Ghost would teach you all things and lead you into all truth.

Think about that *kind* of promise. It's *not* an external miracle that as time wears on people can say, well, God didn't *really* split the Red Sea. It happened like so and so. Or, Jesus wasn't *really* the Son of the Living God. C'mon man, we just *say that stuff to get votes!*

The Holy Ghost, that kind of promise requires that in *truth* my servants actually *experience* for themselves *inside* themselves My presence and the fulfilling of My Word, the fulfilling of Being Goodness inside of them! If that *didn't* happen, there is no way Christianity could have been born. Them trying to *make it up* would have been detected and not have worked because the Promise is not of this world! It's value is *only* for within an individual to experience! Though I *never* told anyone to be a Christian, or a Jew for that matter, I did tell them all to be *holy,* yet, it was the *forerunners* to Christianity, true holy people filled with My Holy Ghost that proved through My Goodness and Power and excellent Wisdom, Understanding, and Love that they had *indeed* received

My Promise. And that was followed up by *many* others receiving that *same* blessing!

It wasn't until all the holy people had been killed off, and a few passed away in old age, that a tremendous mass of people existed, called Christians, that were left with no real example of a holy person to set them straight. Nevertheless, they had Holy Scriptures and there was enough real truth in them for them to support their Christian religions. Their faith is real, it's there, just not fully fulfilled. And many Christians still experience internal blessings that they know are from Me. Contrast *that* love with Islam, because while you are *killing* and *torturing* them, they still love you! So which follower has true life within them? So shall they be your judges.

Actually, what *is* the blessing in spirit that Islam offers to you? Since you *don't* see Me as the Son of God from the beginning of time, then there is *no* new heart and new spirit for you to receive. You cannot receive what you don't believe.

Now, if some of you, *in spite of* your corrupt religion, through the natural goodness I made you out of, if you pray with that goodness to God, I will in fact hear you! If in your hearts it truly is Goodness you are calling to. However, how will you receive much from Me when your dogma stands squarely in the way between you and Me?

Remember, my Promise is to be given *within* you. So prove Me! Ask! I *will* come to you and show you where to begin, how to begin, and why! NO religion can make promises for within you that you *will* experience. Because the followers of a corrupt religion would soon leave after they experience *nothing* except falsely generated personal manifestations. But all of My internal experiences I generate within you are of the Seven Spirits within the One Spirit that I described for you.

WHAT MAJOR RELIGION WAS BORN FROM ...?

Look, you either are able to recognize Goodness for its own sake or you are not, right? And that has to be within you. So ask of Me! You see? You are the *enemy* of My chosen people, yet I extend my hand to you with the desire to bless you. All who fully and truly come to Me will be one holy people together.

This that I have spoken above addresses Muslims of the Middle East. What of the Muslims of other peoples and nations? I ask you, what appeals to you of *that* religion? Compare it to Me! Not to Christianity, though Christianity *is* far superior to Islam. Compare Islam to My Goodness as I have described to you here. As you judge, so shall you be judged. And as I asked above for them to seek Me, I ask and Promise the *same* to you. But I caution you other Muslims. Islam is infected with historical envy, jealousy, and deceit. It *will* infect you with the same, even though *your* historical forefathers had no such heart towards my chosen people the Jews.

CHAPTER 13

THE UNITED STATES POLITICAL LEFT'S GLORIOUS UTOPIAN PLAN

I will focus on the left in the USA, but make no mistake on this, these people are global with a desire for utter global domination. Exceedingly clever, with vast resources, they have studied for decades to reach this very point in time! What did they study? Christians! How to defeat you, and bring down *everything* you own, influence and especially teach. Many decades ago, they made a vow that they would corrupt *everything* about you, rob you of your power and influence, and steal your children right out from under you. Why don't you take a moment and grade their progress over the past sixty years.

And what is their mantra, their *slogan* to convince the world, now? *Inclusivity/Diversity*. What do they teach your little ones? *Diversity makes us stronger?* Really? What makes that true? If you have a *diverse* group of brigands, are they any *less* corrupt due to their diversity? And my kingdom to come which will be made up of every nation and tongue, is it *diversity* that makes it a holy kingdom, or the fact that they *all* turned their back *completely* on the world, gave up their *diversity*, to be one holy nation? And remember what holiness is: *pure* love, life, all goodness. Even I, myself, gave up *my* whole mortal life for goodness sake. *Your* goodness sake!

Make no mistake about this: You cannot become holy if you still see yourself as an ethnic, a religious, or whatever *diversity* label you want. Not black, not white, not even Jew, etc. Why? Because I told you that you *must* forsake *all* for me to give you a new heart and new spirit. I'm not asking you to do *anything* that I haven't done in this process to my *own* mortal self! Deny yourself to receive a new heart and new spirit.

After I ascended to my Father, He reimbued me with my former glory, and with omnipresence, *but* he added to that all the new strength and understanding, all the new goodness I had developed while I was mortal. He incorporated it all into One. What did you think I meant in my prayer when I said, And now, O Father, glorify thou me with thine own self with the glory which I had with thee before the world was. Yes, even I, myself, was given a fully Godly new heart and new spirit by *My* Father! And what do you think I do with you? I take the goodness you are made out of and then integrate *that* with *My* new Heart and Spirit! I don't destroy what you are when you fully give yourself to Me, I make you better as My Father made Me better.

New means *new*. But if your will holds on to *anything* of yourself, I will not give you a new heart and new spirit because I will not force my newness upon you. A new heart and new spirit gives you a completely new identity in Me where holiness is the defining quality, the *uniting* quality.

But what *exactly* do they mean by inclusivity and diversity? They're very good at slight-of-word. Their *Inclusivity* means everyone, *everything* of everyone *except* anything even remotely related to Me,

My Truth, Love, Peace, Wisdom, Understanding, Life, and Justice! Likewise, their *Diversity* means all people and things diverse from Me and Mine! Well, no wonder that makes them stronger!

Sodom and Gomorrah had the *exact* same laws but they included certain *proof of loyalty* edicts which basically required all their citizens to perform *in certain ways,* thereby *ensuring* inclusivity. Only Lot and his daughters had failed to prove their *love.* That's why, when I came down to destroy those cities and all the plain, Lot's sons-in-laws failed to heed Lot's warning to leave. Well, they heard Lot's warning backwards, interpreting it as *mocking Me,* that the city would be destroyed. Hmm, I wonder why they heard the Truth *backwards?* Oh, those two had passed their proof of loyalty tests. And, oh, by the way, the democrats now have proof of loyalty tests, don't they? You can't work, participate in certain needful things unless you bow to them. And, oh, how *hateful* you are if you don't rejoice in trans celebrations. Even President Biden has sworn a public oath to support them, to make them as respected as the best of you. Oh, don't worry, it will get much worse. You *haters* must be made to bow! Or else.

Are you familiar with the lady who worked at one of your Starbucks Coffee Shops? Labored faithfully there for four years. Unfortunately, she was a *Christian* lady, and when she walked into the manager's office, she noticed a box of *company* tea shirts with a very *noble* company logo supporting LGBTQ *pride.* She asked if she would be punished if she didn't wear the shirt, because she was a Christian who believed in what you all now call *traditional family values.* When did you Christians allow MY values to be labeled as *traditional?* Because you know *traditions* fall out of favor over time, *right?*

Oh, that's right, you *Christians* never fought against that label. Why? In fact, is a man and a woman as husband and wife *even a value?* When did you let *that* change of understanding happen? Is the sun rising in the East and setting in the West a *value?* Or is the sky blue, or water *wet,* a *value?* Oh, wait, pardon My *misunderstanding?* Because you have a *will that can choose,* then *everything* about you is a *value?* The fact that you have five fingers on each hand, that's a value? The *fact* that you have a soul, is *that* a *value?* The *fact* that you have a *free will,* is *that* a value? The *fact* that a man has a *penis* is *that* a *value?* How about a woman's vagina? How about a man's testicles or a woman's ovaries? True, they all have value but that's different than calling them a *value,* a mere principle you decide to hold to or *change.*

Oh, I see, you had no *choice* over that, the way you came into the world, but some of you are *trying* to create your choice of what you are made to be, so you think *anything* you can choose is a *value?* Well, you can *choose* to cut off your arm or even your stones, for that matter, does that make *them* into a *value?* True, you have deemed them *valueless,* but that foolishness doesn't work in reverse to claim these things are mere *values!* And what do you get when a male human or female human decides to destroy their masculinity or femininity?

The left tells you that a male lacking masculinity is a female and a female lacking femininity is a male. That's like saying a zirconium is a diamond, but what happens when you smash a zirconium with a hammer? You *cannot* create femininity in a man by destroying his masculinity because femininity is purely and strictly a defining natural *quality* of being *female*. Destroying masculinity in a man and causing himself to act *effeminate* is a display *lacking* righteous strength, righteous aggression, righteous authority, righteous sureness, righteous assertiveness, righteous cherishing of the more refined part of the human being that he is *not,* that being the woman, and righteous responsibility of being made first, before the woman, and therefore needful to face dangers *first*. Note the word *righteous*. Because as the Beast rises, he will *proudly* assert himself being most evil!

Why did I make the man and his masculinity *first*? Because it was right and needful to first set the Earthly godly standard, to have *that* strength, surety, the will to *act* certainly without delay in place *before* I brought forth that which would refine that standard into a gold standard, which would balance strength with tenderness, and enhance surety of a staunch position and immediate and direct action with consideration of the overall effects of that orientation and how to bring an extra grace to it. The saying that a man provides the house but his wife turns it into a home has foundational depth that is *not* a value, but is as the sky is blue and water wet, dear Christians!

What *effeminate* is *not,* is a natural nurturing felt in the depths of a woman's bosom and her 'gut.' Effeminate is *not* the natural feminine call and longing to nurture, nor is it the natural studious desire to refine the male world into something more *balanced*. *Effeminate* doesn't possess the special wisdom I embedded into femininity that automatically sees *exactly* where and how to support the masculine. *Effeminate* cannot complete the complementary unity with masculinity because at the heart of *effeminity* is destruction whereas the heart of femininity is nurturing life and strength, and refining the standard into a *gold* standard, so to speak.

Why do you think that after I created the first woman, I said, and behold, it was *very* good? Nowhere else did I say that. Because the true man and woman *together* are the free complementary unity in God's image as My Father and I are One in Freedom. The very basis of the Essence of All Realities, physical and spiritual, in Heaven and on Earth! Complementary unity. *That's* how important true masculinity and femininity are for *you*, if you want to be real and not self-destructive at the most fundamental level. There is no destruction in true femininity because there is no destruction in Me, but there *is* full destruction in *effemininity*. And the same is true for women destroying their femininity which *appears* to be masculinity but it's *not*.

Was I not allowed to make one woman for one particular man? Was I not allowed to make them the perfect complement to each other thus forming the perfect *free* unity of oneness? Or do you prefer and imagine hopefully for discord? Do you lie awake at night hoping for the one who will irritate and upset you?

Was I *not* allowed to fashion their oneness after the perfect *free* Unity of Oneness I have with God Almighty, my Father? Is My Unity or the unity I created for man and woman a mere *value?* Or is it the reflection of the very *Essence of Reality* that *I AM?* Just like all My Creation reflects Our Goodness in infinite ways. True, there is true *value* in all of it because it all has true *meaning*. Don't confuse that value with *values* you hold as mere beliefs or principles and therefore you have a right to change them. Why am I focusing on this perversion when I have titled this chapter United States Political Left's Utopian Plan? You'll see.

Christians, you should have been wiser, you should have known better and known how to protect society against such abomination. Remember how I explained Lucifer who became Satan in an earlier chapter? He is quite adept at bait and switch and redefining *everything*. Do you see the *power* in his tricks and how they *rob* you of your power? Just because you can choose something, *anything,* and by virtue of such a choice a value is implicitly given to the object of your choice, *that* doesn't mean that *object* is a value! Marriage between a man and a woman is *not* a value. It *is* part of the very structure of your reality of goodness! Choosing *whom* to marry places different

UNITED STATES POLITICAL LEFT'S UTOPIAN PLAN

value on prospective mates in *relation to* choosing, but *having a mate* is *not* part of the value system. There is one for each of you. In other words, it is *insanity* or extreme wickedness to even *think* you can be god over your structure and then deem yourselves with the power to change it into something that remains good. And remember, I made you free out of what you *already were* when you were inside of me! And then, with that freedom you want self-destruction? You *hate* the goodness you were in the beginning?

Are *you* God? Tell me how you created the atom and then put them together in myriad ways. Tell Me how you created gravity, or spirit, or how Goodness is omnipresent, then I will confess to you that you have a *right* to change My Creation and call *that* change good. Other than that, all that you do in this fashion is pure evil of the highest degree. Why the highest? Because there are many sins that do *not* change My Creation, such as stealing and lying. True, they corrupt the soul, they bring harm, *but* they do *not* change the actual structure! The soul that sins, is *still* a soul, just a corrupted one. But *what* are you when you change your very structure, as in homosexuals, trans-sexuals, or whatever other perversions you can imagine? You have stepped *outside* the very Essence of Reality, not just by sinning, but also by changing structure! You have gone from being a human being to a human *beast,* just as Lucifer became Satan.

Look, I desire that you understand the utter depths of this kind of sin and why it provoked me to utterly burn up Sodom and Gomorrah. Consider an artist, a painter who paints a perfect picture on the canvas. There are two types of corruption to the picture and the one type the artist can correct but the other he cannot correct and must discard the whole thing! Corruptions to the image on the canvass, like sins of stealing, lying, even *murder,* can be repented for, the image can be corrected. *But,* corruption to the very canvass itself upon which the picture rests, *that* cannot be fixed! No matter what picture you paint on it, no matter your effort of will or your *value system,* the canvass is corrupt and by that, the picture is corrupt.

The class of perversions I described corrupt the canvas. How can you be forgiven for that, *if* you corrupt the canvas, if you as a man or a woman wipe out your natural desire for the opposite gender and turn it towards the same gender, or if you attempt to change your gender, or if you alter yourselves in other perverted ways? Oh, by the way, when I say gender, I mean the sex you were born with.

You have destroyed yourselves. If you murder, you can repent for that because you still have a *structure* that allows for redemption. But if you have *destroyed* the structure inherent in the soul, whether it be a masculine soul or a feminine soul, not just the body, well, you are not the Creator, and you have no power to restore that which you lost! And the kind of choice you made to finalize your own destruction in body and soul, I cannot go against your choice, because the *structure,* I only create *once!* Even I only had One structure, one mortal life, one mortal masculine soul, one mortal body! You change that structure from a human being to a human *beast,* you have committed suicide and that is *not* forgivable. In fact, don't you tell everyone it's an *orientation,* not just a choice? You have spoken truly. It *is* what you have become but I only forgive human beings, not human *beasts.*

Some of you might say that, well, the canvass can be repaired, too. How? You didn't make it. And while a soul can repent from non-structural sins like murder, even rape, understand what that process of repentance is. It is turning completely away from the evil whereupon the picture on the canvass is fixed and aligned with the goodness of your repentance. A murderer, when repenting, drives murder completely from their being when asking for forgiveness, they feel they are not worthy to live, and the same is true for all repentable sins as their goodness cries unto me. You and I are both operating *together* within that image on the canvass.

But, if you destroy the canvass, it no longer feels natural, *does it?* Where do you then get the natural feeling you need to offset against the unnatural in order to repent to have the canvass mended? Can you drive homosexuality completely out so that you can truly repent? To do so you need to find that which is naturally against it within you, you need to find somewhere in you that has no feeling of homosexuality *at all*. But the canvas is broken and that break creates the perverse feeling. The soul of a murderer yet possesses both good and evil and so the good can reach for repentance. How does the destroyed canvass reach for that which has not been destroyed because your destruction permeates the *whole* canvass. That's why it's an *orientation.* How does someone who killed themselves turn back time? They can't.

And *if* you reached for my forgiveness, well, how would you do that? You have to give everything of being a human *being* back to me. And even *if* you gave me your *orientation,* how would you give back the *being* part when it no longer exists in you? And if the being part *does* still exist, then you are saying there is a part of you that is *not* homosexual or perverse? Hmmmm . . .

Notice that the *structure* of being a male soul or a female soul is innate, as innate as the uniqueness of me or my Father, *each* as free, inimitable *individual* parts of the Trinity with *different* structures after which I modeled the man and the woman, masculinity and femineity.

And just as my desire is always to the Father and his to me, so is the innate structure of the man and the woman *in their souls* and bodies, in their masculinity and femininity. And even some of you Christians misunderstand this because you read the letters saying there is no male nor female, no Greek nor Jew before God. That is in relation to how my Justice and Love treats every soul, treats the *picture* on the canvass. And to be clear, whether male or female, if you destroy the canvass, you also will be treated the same by me.

So, it will not, *should not* surprise anyone that *Diversity* and *Inclusion* is well supported by what you call your LGBT community. In fact, you will find them at the very heart of all your leftist organizations. And their *primary goal?* Oh, I need to finish the story about the Christian lady. She asked if she would be punished if she didn't wear the LGBT *pride* shirt, because she was a Christian who believed in what you all now call *traditional family values*. Her manager told her she wouldn't be punished. A short while later, she was fired. That shouldn't come as a surprise that the Left's deepest felt desire for you is that you can't work, can't earn a living, can't do *anything* but suffer until you recant your *vile, hate filled, unjust, perverse* faith and belief in Me! Sound backwards? I wonder why.

And something else to note: In her legal statement she said she had *nothing* against LGBTQ, but she just supported *Biblical Teachings* that one man is for one woman and that sex outside of marriage is shunned. You know, when I was here on Earth, I groaned. It's written once, but actually, I groaned a lot. I do so now because the perverted seem to be *smarter* than the *Christians!*

The Christian woman said she has nothing against the LGBTQ and yet she knows the Holy Bible that she loves has countless instances where I, or I had others completely destroy those people. Now, the perverted know this, and they take that more seriously than you do! In other words, they understand *clearly* the threat to their existence and that if you *truly* love Me and you're not a fool, you're going to despise the perverse, too, because their normalization is *your* destruction. Aren't they now passing laws all over the world that will fine you or *jail you* if you speak against the perverse? But they can speak against you with impunity and without danger?

Oh, wait, I know what Christians are taught: Hate the sin but love the sinner, *right*? Except: Do you remember of old, as in the Old Testament, that there were seven nations that I commanded the children of Israel to utterly destroy and don't even touch *any* of their wealth, but gather it into the center of their cities and burn it! Do you Christians assume that, well, *that* was back then, but *not* now? So, I guess then, you ignore the Scripture that says, What has been, will be? I destroyed those *kind* of sinners because I had no Love left for them because they had unforgivably blasphemed against My Spirit and drove all goodness from themselves, just as in the days of Noah where every thought and imagination of their hearts was only evil *continually*. Yes, that's a quote from *My* Holy Scriptures.

And the *Perverse* know without any doubt they are unforgivable, and so when they look at you *Christians,* they see only fools, lambs for the slaughter. And yet, you *Christians,* most of you, are clueless! Why? Because you haven't received the full blessing I described to you earlier in this *fiction*. You know how the *Christians* of old, not the holy people who were before them, you know how those Christians sort of puffed themselves up by railing against the Jews' unbelief? They felt so far superior to My chosen people because they fell but the Christians rose. Well, dear *Christians,* are you not making the *exact* same mistake as the Jews did when I told them *not* to make any allegiance with those condemned nations? And yet, there you are, showing *love* to them, making what you call *friendships,* and being so *very* careful to explain that *you* don't condemn them, *you* don't have *anything against them at all* . . . except that you despise their lifestyle!

Oh, wait, *despise* might be too strong a word. Let's soften that. Let's leave *you* out of it all together. The *Bible* doesn't approve of such things. And *why?* Well, the *Perverse* will tell *you* the Truth. The Bible explicitly describes a fierce hated for them. Let me tell *you* the Truth, too, dear *Christians*. You who have called yourselves *Christians* to imply that you have some likeness to Me. If My Holy Ghost is in you, you *will* utterly despise the perverse. They will make your very flesh crawl, and you will cringe inside at the spiritual stench of them, and my *wrath* will burn hot inside you, of which you will have to keep to yourselves because even holy people, they aren't *the* Judge of all, though I do have *holy* people to issue my judgments, and on occasion, even call down plagues upon mankind, but when *I* tell them to. That's why even the angels I sent to Sodom did *not* destroy any of the provocateurs who accosted them and Lot's family *before* they had left Sodom. It wasn't time. They were just smote with blindness so the righteous could escape.

Yes, if you *Christians* have detected my anger toward you, you would be correct. Consider that I also had, and still have, quite a bit of anger toward my chosen people, the Jews. They carry *My* name, right? But then again, don't *you* now also carry *My* name? Come to Me, Christians, more deeply than you have before, and allow me to teach you what you needed to know quite a while ago! I will show you inside yourselves the Truth, and *why* it's True beyond any doubts!

So, you have now, very powerful and wealthy companies doing things like not allowing people who sell firearms to use their credit cards, their banks. If you hold certain *conservative* views, you may not be allowed to speak openly *in the USA* in certain places, nor attend certain schools, enter certain professions. . . . well, the list keeps growing. And Oh, all that money I bless you with for retirement? A lot of it now goes to ESG companies which make sure to invest *your* money into *woke* causes and corporations, no matter whether there is financial gain or not. And, Oh, almost forgot to mention that in many of your *elementary schools,* your *teachers* are asking *your* children to closely evaluate their sexuality and gender, two *different* things to them, and these *teachers* are dutifully explaining the difference, as, of course, your children are *curious.* And, since you hate the sin but *love* the sinner, they also tell your children to love them and not to look down upon them, not to be *haters*. They *also* tell them it is *normal* to have perverted feelings and thoughts and give them a brief description about what that might look like. They *also* tell them to be on the lookout for such feelings and thoughts and don't be ashamed to embrace them, don't be ashamed of who you are, little children. And after this *set up,* Satan joyfully brings them the thoughts and feelings. Is it any wonder that a third of certain elementary students in certain classes now identify as LGBTQ? Oh, you *Christians* just keep loving the perverse but hate the sin, OK? And you looked down upon the Jews because *they* fell? But *some* of you Christians think *you* have it all right and you will be fine without all the rest, *right?* So the Jews that were faithful to me when Israel fell were *alright?*

I told you that a house divided will *not* stand. The Left is well united in their *hatred* for you. How well are all Christians coming together and even discussing what is happening? What are your plans to work together, to build your *own* economy within which you can function freely? How would you even do that? Oh, you are praying and waiting for *Me* to fix it? The things open to *your* will are *yours* to fix, not Mine, just like they were for Israel. Consider this work of *fiction* a blessing for you.

The LGBTQ community is quite small, a people who used to have no power and historically shunned by every single nation and people on Earth. Quite a feat for them to have the power and support they have now. They hitched a ride in your sixty's civil rights era and *came out of the closet.* Other minorities, *ethnic* minorities began to accept them in a common fight, which at the time, was indeed a true fight for justice. But where ethnic minorities led by Martin Luther King and others demanded that the USA step up and recognize them as human beings, that other people *come up to MLK's level,* that of acting as and *being* a just human being, that same message twisted inside-out as applied to the LGBTQ community. Not only that, MLK was a serious *Christian* preacher quite unlike the race baiters hiding in MLK's shadow. Yes, these so-called *shadow* preachers, who were not even worthy to be in MLK's shadow, have laid claim to a certain culture! Shame on you for accepting them and giving them *anything* at all.

Those shadow-loving so-called preachers fit in much better with LGBTQ because their hearts are dark, filled with hate for Me, and lustful for power and influence. Once MLK was assassinated, gone was his peaceful movement. Gone was the call for all people to join together in Godly love where no one was judged by the color of their skin or other *innocent* characteristics. What took its place?

So-called black militants turned MLK's message upside down and his love into hate. Along with that came illicit drugs and unbridled sexual behavior into the black community. Illegitimacy rates in the black community, which were low back then, skyrocketed. Personal responsibility as a *value* was replaced by blaming others. The 'shadow preachers' and others needed force behind this blame so they could enrich themselves and shake down businesses. Now, today, Critical Race Theory is becoming a gold standard in HR departments across the USA within and outside the government. The theory religiously preaches *Inclusion/Diversity* and heaps on *white guilt.*

Now, instead of viewing what *you* call *black* people as human beings, you want them first and foremost recognized as *black.* I can't tell you how *repulsive* this is to Me! What *value* is there in a skin color or even ethnicity? To my *own* chosen people, the Jews of old, I told them: Be confounded for your pride! And then I described to them the curses that would befall them. If I so punished *My chosen,* what will I do to you *blacks?* Do you *blacks* even want to know the truth about your skin color? Which of Noah's three sons did you come from? Well, why don't you first look at your *arrogance* and then pick which son! Then maybe you won't so *foolishly* praise your skin color. And even just maybe, you'll be wise and not have it be important to you at all.

Tell me, does Love belong to a *skin color* or *any* ethnic group, or is it Mine, Mine to give to accepting *souls* which is what gives them their *being*? How about Justice? You love to shout, No Justice, No Peace. Well, Peace is mine, too. And when you shout that, you are not talking about justice, nor peace, you are declaring war on your enemies with *vengeance.* Didn't I tell everyone that Vengeance *also* belongs to me? Most notably, the Marxist founders of BLM are of the LGBTQ community. Well, what a coincidence! How shocking. And since the conscience of so many in the black community has been so very bruised, *or even destroyed,* it's so easy for them to be used as stupid *pawns,* just like the founders of communism used the ignorant masses and then *enslaved* them all after they took power.

You might be wondering why I sound so, well, biting. Wasn't the Lord Jesus all about *love?* Ahh, you see, again, your enemies want you to stick with that. They want you to *love* them, but *not* the way

I meant it for you! Their desire for you to *love* them means for you to stay the hell out of their way so they can grow more powerful and rule over you and persecute you, and generally have fun with your suffering. When I told you to love your enemies, I *didn't* have *that* in mind. And the reason I sound so biting? Why does My Anger burn hotter and hotter?

To every season there is a purpose under Heaven. Right? You Christians are stuck on the *previous* season, because all you pretty much do is read but take little guidance from my Holy Ghost concerning the *present!* Remember, Revelations shows you that as My Father did in the Old Testament, I will do in the New! Now do you understand My Anger? And I am particularly angry at you, because I *do* love you with a special love that I *don't* have for many others! You can be *much better* than you are now, and you *need to be.*

So, what do BLM and all the other leftists in the world hate? Judeo/Christian values, *traditional* family values, everything associated with *Me!* Behold, I have heard you *Leftists!* Your chants have reached into Heaven, and I am considering you. It is true that there is no Peace without My Justice.

Tell Me, all you who call yourselves *black* and have pride in such a vanity, who forced you to debase yourselves, to mistreat your women and children? Who forced your men not to honor their women by *being* a good husband to the mother of *their* children? Who forced your women to open their legs and bear children to different men, and none of them your husbands? Who forced you to put that poison in your veins, up your noses, and to debase yourselves beyond even an animal recognition! You think I don't see you, *all* of you? And don't tell me that *white* people do the same things, because they *don't!* They don't make a political movement out of their *debauchery* and then call

UNITED STATES POLITICAL LEFT'S UTOPIAN PLAN

it their *culture!* And then *demand* that everyone *respect* it! Oh, wait, *liberal* white people do. As I said, *Surely,* I have heard you! All of you.

But *you,* who call yourselves *black,* or you are far left, do you want Me to tell you more truth about yourselves? You have so lowered yourselves beyond human recognition so that rather than be honest, humble, and repent to Me that I might heal you and give you back dignity, you treasure up your *hatred* and *vengeance* as if it were the best nutrition. You are drunk with your thievery, illicitness, hatred, and your senses are so dull that *anyone* or *anything* easily manipulates you to their own purposes regardless of what harm might come to you. To those *behind* your scenes, *you* are fools and expendable. You are fodder for them, and once they are in power, you will do as you are commanded to do, or else! You thought black slavery was bad? You fools! You *wretched* fools. Maybe you should give Me a second and third thought instead of feeding the wave of the *Beast* you are now riding because the *Beast* is your new International Rules Based Order!

And then you have other assorted *minorities.* That's what they like to call themselves in the USA. It engenders compassion from the not so bright liberal women who help vote in useful idiots. But *back home* where *some* of those assorted minorities come from, well, they are not loved so much because a lot of them *are* criminals! And what is the enemy of criminals? Law and order. So the *Beast* will have you destroy law and order either through foolish policies, more brazen criminals that overwhelm officers of the law, and through them flat out quitting this noble profession that *I* called them to! And then you have other minorities who fondly hearken back unto faded history when they were *pagans* and they remember a faded time when *they* ruled the land of the America's. And so, when they see the great prosperity of the USA, well, they get a bit jealous, and so they match up quite well with the so-called *black* and *perverse* vengeance seekers!

And lastly, in dealing with *minorities*- and by the way, I'm *sarcastic* when using that word because I despise the concept. In the USA there is a founding principle that Justice is blind. *That* came from My Holy Scriptures saying, Thou shalt not respect the person of the rich nor the poor, but in righteousness thou shalt judge. Odd there wasn't even a single mention of *race*. Why? Race is *irrelevant* to Me. Moses wife was Ethiopian. When I was angry at the children of Israel in the desert, after I had brought them out of the land of Egypt, I told Moses to stand aside and let Me destroy them in the moment because they are a stiff-necked, rebellious people, and I would make Moses into a great nation. As I said, his *wife* was Ethiopian. But Moses withstood Me, saying, Then what will the other nations say of You, that You brought out this great people to destroy them.

Moses wasn't thinking, Ahh, yes, let's have *blacker* inheritors to God's blessings! All he was thinking is how best to glorify Goodness, which I AM. And *that* is how I approach every single living soul on an *individual* basis. *Where* is My goodness in them? What condition is it in? And what blessings are they able to receive, if *any*?

Now, with that said, lastly, in dealing with *minorities, besides* those I already described, there are also many peoples from different nations who come to the USA, many illegally. For them, they feel it is in their best interest for the *Democrats* to be in power. It doesn't matter to these illegals if that destroys souls on a mass level. It doesn't matter to these illegals if abominable policies are greatly furthered by their support, and *sometimes* even voting when they aren't allowed. It doesn't matter to these *illegals* if the democrats *use them* by furthering the lie that President Trump is a racist because he wants to halt illegal immigration. *And,* it doesn't matter to these illegals that the fact is they do *not* deserve to be citizens in a country where they came in *illegally,* that is, it doesn't matter that they break the law and destabilize aspects of the country. These illegals would be quite happy to be given citizenship and quite happy to repay the Democrats with their votes. Why? Why are they happy even when most of them happen to have more *conservative* feelings and values about life? Quite simply, they are looking out for number one, themselves. Put a different way, they are *selfish,* and don't give a *damn* about the harm they do to a *foolish* country who would let them in, in the first place!

So for *them,* they may have *conservative* values but that's *only* for them, to *hell* with everyone else! Well, I'm sorry to tell you that in *Reality* it doesn't quite work out that way. Don't forget My promise to the whole world, I will render unto *everyone* according as their work shall be, and has been. Do you *selfish* people feel good about that? And by the way, why did you leave your homes to come to the USA? For a better life for yourselves? Oh, I believe that. But, wait a minute. Some of your countries down south have almost *half* your population living up *north* in the USA! Well, are you telling Me that you so *destroyed* your own country that you had to come up to the USA to destroy her?

And you say, No, no. I don't want her destroyed. I *need* her. And I left home because of very bad people there. Except, one little thing bothers Me *greatly.* When you leave your home in such *great* numbers because you say you are fleeing evil, isn't that also saying you are *cowards?* That, rather than stand up against evil in the home you *love,* you'd rather just give up and flee. But, and think about this *very* carefully, isn't this the *exact* same thing you are doing in the USA? You *know* without *any* doubt that the *Democrats* are using you for evil intent, but rather than stand up against it, you just act like it doesn't affect you. In other words, you *run* from your *moral* responsibilities just like you did back home. Right? And you *really* think this will work out well for you and your children? Think again! You already know what socialism is and does to *you!*

And *then,* after *all this* I described, you have a very sophisticated and *very* wise nation, people, and country, which is China. They have *six and a half billion* people and far many more men than women because, basically, they murdered their daughters, mostly unborn, because they like boys more. Now, in ancient times, this kind of problem, not having enough women for the men, was easily solved by simply conquering other countries, killing or enslaving their men, and taking their women for wives. Six and a half *billion.*

Now China has a vast and ancient history, and in *their* eyes, the West hasn't had much influence on them for very long. What's a few hundred years to thousands? Now they, too, see your debauchery in the West, and if possible, they are truly glad to aid the groups responsible for much of it! They will buy up as many of your politicians as possible. They might even let a virus or two *accidently* escape their land to wreak utter havoc on western economies. True, some of their vast population dies, but *everyone* dies, and besides, the Great Wall of China has untold numbers of forced labor buried beneath it. A *Great Civilization* knows how to make sacrifices for the greater good.

Oh, by the way, the Chinese utterly *detest* the West's perversities! If *they* ruled the West, well, none of *that* would exist. That's what they joke about in private to themselves, how that they encourage debasement in the West, in the USA especially, and how, once they take over, how they will 'remove it' from existence. Oh, and *no* amount of pleading, begging, liberal crying will move them one iota. You see, they know from *their* ancient history and philosophy that when human beings in a country lower themselves into the slime pit, *that* civilization cannot last long. Why do you think in ancient times they developed their traditions and philosophy? And why do you think they have *moral police* to make sure their people stay in line now?

As the founders of the United States constitution told you, the destruction of America will not come from an external enemy, it will be from within. China understands this. Their ancient culture understands war better than anyone. Their ancient tome, The Art of War, though quite small, has giant understanding and is very clear on how to win a bloodless battle.

And *finally,* behind the scenes you have those *geniuses* of whom I spoke in the beginning of this work of *fiction.* Their roots are in with the sixties dope head culture, cocaine users – not crack, that's for dumb n-… these *geniuses* founded *tech* companies and have become the richest most powerful businesses in the world. And let Me tell you, they are sincerely *impressed* by all the tech and abilities they have created, or paid someone else to create. Every day there's a new discovery yielding even more power and influence. And the beauty of this? It's so complicated only a select few really understand it, which *means* that if you are using their tech to, let's say, run election counting, well, just trust them. They will do the *right* thing. And *that* makes them even more drunk with the *true* power behind the scenes.

Now these *geniuses* actually have something very much in common with all the lowly *grunts on the ground.* These *geniuses* have a *very* sick conscience, too. So they are *simpatico* with their little minions like BLM, ANTIFA, and other rioters, basically the cannon fodder for a future revolution. A revolution where they, the *geniuses,* will have to step up and bring order to. Who else? They've paid off the leaders, too, on every side. Oh, wait, not *quite* simpatico, because *they,* the *geniuses,* live behind walls and gates, and have security forces to protect them . . . from what?

But you see, *they* have the resources everyone will need once the *revolution* collapses the economy, *destroys* the USA as you now know it, and of course, China, being the compassionate country, in which these *geniuses* also are *heavily* invested in, well, China will be more than glad to help the *new* USA, one that will understand the Chinese good nature and *their* needs. Hmm, now what happens to that *fly-over* country? You know, the people with no say, no power except President Trump gave them a *glimmer* of hope that just couldn't be allowed to stand.

Well, the Chinese had to deal with these kinds of private problems. Even back then, they still had a lot of people, a lot of people who thought they owned their *own* land, for instance. The Chinese leaders took care that. They will *help* in any way they can to *help* the USA *revolution,* the *new* USA, to take care of all those *selfish* people who don't understand that the land, *everything* pretty much, belongs to *all* the people, not just a select few! And, the *new* USA, will represent *all* the people . . . ahh, just not Christians. And the *new* government? Well, they *will be* the voice for *all* the people. And don't worry if you don't like that. You will, or else. Now, doesn't that just sound so absolutely *wonderful?* Why don't you all celebrate it now? It's coming. And by the way? The Chinese *know* that the very *best* race on Earth is . . . wait for it . . . the Chinese, *particularly* the *lighter* color Chinese. Has *always* been that way.

What a Utopia, right? You have *no* idea, yet. And the good news? Those so-called *geniuses* have no idea *either!* They *think* they *know,*

UNITED STATES POLITICAL LEFT'S UTOPIAN PLAN

but they don't. They don't want to know this, and I'm *not* going to tell them. They'll find out soon enough.

Oh, and one more thing? Who is making all this wonderful progress possible? Well, in order for this *progress* to happen in a nation who *overwhelmingly* voted *legally* for President Donald Trump, well, the *geniuses* had to have a secure, safe place in which to 'set the election right.' In fact, in Philadelphia, the head of Facebook bought the voting machines, paid the election workers, dictated the rules and drop box positions and how many there should be, and they did this all within a generous *charitable* four-hundred-million-dollar donation to the battleground states with stipulations just named to all of them!

But the *real* key here was that these places where they tallied the votes were in what you call the heart of the ghetto where the racist, white hating, USA hating African Americans who *call themselves* niggers, are in control. And control they did, no matter the objection of the few poll watchers that bravely managed to be there. What did the *African Americans* do to the objectors? They threw them out, blocked their view and *even* cheered and mocked them when they were thrown out. In short, they used *force* to cheat! And since they *rule* the ghetto along with the billionaire big tech leaders, there was absolutely *nothing* that good Christians could do, at least from *their* limited perspective.

The irony of this I do not want to escape My readers of this work of *fiction*. The most so-called underprivileged, the *lowest*, the *basest*, the acclaimed biggest *victims* of white, Christian hate and evil oppression, the *African Americans who call themselves niggers* ended up having all the power to change the course of the USA, and by *that*, the course of the whole world! Well, looks like their *hatred*, desire for *vengeance*, and greater desire to blame *anyone* else for their failures *but themselves,* well, their desire is fulfilled, isn't it? You are so *very* powerful now and *important,* aren't you? Doesn't that make you feel on top of the world, you who call yourselves *niggers,* who helped steal the election away from the one man who lifted up minority economic status more than any other President? Please don't worry, don't have a care, the Chinese are cheering for you, and they have *utter* contempt for you and plan on dealing with you once they win. But will they? Because the Beast has his most major investments here in the West!

Want more irony? The Chinese hate the Beast's main play thing, the LGBT folks. And *that* is a bit of a problem for the Beast, because as it tells you in Daniel, he shall not regard the desire of women! That's a quote from My Holy Scriptures. Ohhh, what is a Beast to do. His grand dreams are to invert *all* of my structure, to bring it all down into utter perverseness. He *can't* have a country like China going around with *morality* police, telling her men to be more masculine, more manly, even if they are atheistic! Because, in truth. The Chinese are too . . . wait for it. . . too Godly to allow *them* to rule the world! So, even though the Chinese are doing everything they can to aid the Beast in destroying the USA, the Chinese are in fact giving strength to the Beast who will destroy them!

Want more irony? There is one group in the whole world, one geographic area who can actually greatly hinder the Beast and forestall his rule for quite a while. The very people the Chinese have undermined both in their country and the USA. Conservative Christians! The Bible Belt. The 'Red' states in the USA! If only they could understand what they need to do.

So now, what is the Judge of all Heaven and Earth to do? How about write you the Truth in a work of *fiction?* Now, what are you going to do with it? I've been judging souls and nations and angels from the beginning of time. Do you understand what that means at all? It means, once I judge you, *that* is your future for *eternity*. Now do you understand why I am so patient, why I let you go so far down the hole that you can't even see any light above? Because that is *your* time where your *free will* can truly matter. I don't interfere with it. I call on souls to do good, but it's up to them!

CHAPTER 14

WHAT CAN BE DONE TO DELAY THE BEAST?

I can't just tell you all that I have had written here without giving you an effective solution to the Beast that seeks to devour you. As it was in King Josiah's time where he humbled himself to me and I told him I would not bring Israel's destruction in his lifetime *that I was about to bring,* so can it be today if only. . .

You conservative Christian supposed-to-be *pastors, leaders, protectors of your flock,* if you can find it in your hearts to take seriously what I said in My Holy Scriptures, *you* can forestall the Beast for a good while. That would give you and the world more time to repent, to gain righteous strength. Didn't I tell you that a house divided will not stand? Then what in the *hell* are you doing? Are you all together? Conservative Baptists, Methodist, Pentecostals, and, *yes,* conservative Catholics, too, as well as other conservatives, you all have far more in common with each other than the liberals within your own denominations sent there to poison you. But all of you are scattered about. Your resources, your lands, your wealth is all scattered about.

And while you do manage to vote together, that isn't anywhere near enough strength to face what is coming, and, in fact, what is already here, and you *know* it.

As I said earlier, if you are waiting on Me to fix this for you, you had better think again. What has already been given to you to be able to *fix this yourselves,* is in *your* hands to do, *not* Mine. All that wealth and resource you have, did *you* get that? Are you praising yourself, or is it I, your Lord God who gave you power to get wealth? So why don't you all be wise and use your wealth and resources to come together and unite to protect what you all love in common? Amongst conservatives, no matter your religious denomination, you have so much more in common than not. So what should you do?

You have something unique in the whole world, a geographic location where most of you are but now not nearly enough. Still, it *is* your home, even home to those conservatives who don't live there but if they came, they would agree they are home. The Bible Belt, the 'Red States' and even Pennsylvania which is, in fact Red, but stolen. In this dire case for the world, *geography* matters. Strategy *matters.* Fighting *the* War wisely, matters. Why?

Because the Beast is pulling all his resources together to destroy you. Social media, social workers, most news outlets, education, government, banks, stock market, nations of liberals, and enemies of the USA, all together to destroy you poor lil' conservative Christians, and yet they fear you! Because they *know* you still have the resources to withstand even all of them! But they also know, frankly, that you're stupid and they intend to keep you that way. But I am here, now, to give you wisdom.

Why did the Trucker's Strike in Canada scare the ruling class and libs? Because the truckers, who are also mostly you, control

WHAT CAN BE DONE TO DELAY THE BEAST?

a valuable resource and shut so much down when they used their power. Did you know that almost half the monetary support for them came from you conservatives? Unfortunately, there is no one religious denomination, nor single segment of economic control that is strong enough to win this war. And Canada has no Bible Belt, a geographic location for conservatives to call home. So they are subject everywhere to liberal governance, the governance of the Beast. So the Truckers Strike failed, but worse, because now the Canadian government is going after them and their supporters and they have no defense.

What do conservatives and Christians mostly control? Lumber? Cement? Block and other building supplies? Most blue collar workers are now conservative. Food! Most farmers are conservative and Christian. Energy like oil and gas? And transportation like trucks and trains.

Can the libs even live without you? Even survive? Why do you think their policies attack farmers? Now nitrogen, the key ingredient in fertilizer, is environmentally dangerous and in need of regulation? The farmers in Holland had a huge protest about it but they can't win because liberal governance extends throughout Holland and the libs need to control such a vital resource. The Environmental Protection Agencies across the world are weaponized to control your resources. How are you farmers in California doing? Bit of a water shortage have you? How much of it goes to save a few fish by EPA decree? Oh, there's so much more *purposefully* destroying you.

What if conservatives all pulled out of the deep blue states like California and New York and took all their wealth, their businesses, their families and moved to the Bible Belt and other Red States? What if our truckers stopped trucking into blue cites like LA, Philadelphia, Chicago, NYC, San Francisco, and others? But wait. Let's not be so harsh but wise. We won't cut them off completely. Let's build huge warehouses outside their city limits and we'll truck to there because it's *too dangerous* to truck into those cities any more, and then make them pick up their own 'damned' food! And of course, we'll need to charge them a warehouse fee. We might even have special truckers to go from the warehouses into the city but that would really cost them if they wanted that. Let's suck out every nickel, dime, penny from the blue states that we can!

Hmmm, building materials like lumber and others. What if we prioritized conservative states first. We're going to need a lot of supplies to support the influx of conservative people. Let's operate all energy distribution out from conservative states with all control centered there.

You might ask how could we get people to cooperate to do such a tremendous thing? Ahhh, that's where the pastors, your so-called religious leaders come in. They know their congregations, the resources within them, and they know likeminded people. The pastors are in a very unique and needful position so that if they all could be brought together then my Holy Spirit could show them how to cooperate and help each other. 'Hey, I hate farming in California but where would I go?' one farmer might say. 'Hey, there's a thousand acres right in Tennessee. Jim over there was gonna try and make a killing on it but let me talk to him. He's a good Christian and I think he'd be willing to sell at a good price for you because he'd rather see it go to you than China or Bill Gates.

Do you even know how many abandoned homes, buildings, farms, factories there are across the red states? There is plenty of room for such an exodus. And instead of bringing huge factories, split them up into smaller ones and scatter them through the Red State small towns so if a disease comes again, you won't have to shut large factories down. And smaller factories will help preserve your culture more so than huge ones with a huge influx of folks crowding into a small area.

The wisdom, the knowledge, the talent to do all that I just described and *much* more *is already with you!* You just don't know it yet because you haven't come together, yet, like you should, like you *must* if you want to survive longer. And what are the benefits to accomplishing all this?

If you pull your resources together to protect what you all love in common that means a very sizable part of the United States economy dealing with essential goods and services will be geographically stationed in states solidly in conservative control. That means liberal *state* laws and law enforcement cannot be used to force you into a corner. But also importantly is that conservative states can then resist your federal laws that infringe upon *your* rights. You see? I'm trying to help you avoid an all out civil war by using the law of strength as President Trump often explained to you.

Once you consolidate your resources that the blue states and reprobates cannot do without, then when they order you to call Jane by the name of Jim or Jim by the name of Ruth, or whatever, or they order you to perform abortions and many other destructive evil things they have in mind, you simply tell them, No!

They will try and force the matter, but even if they stack your supreme court and your senate, you plainly tell them, "We've had enough. We're not going to live like that, nor put up with it any more. Do you want to eat? Do you want to keep warm in the winter, cool in the summer? Do want your goods and services to be transported to you effectively and timely? Leave us alone! Just like that song Progress by John Rich, "If you leave us alone, we'll be just fine."

Now, the wisdom in all this is that if your enemy says they will attack you, you say, "And how will that feed you and keep you warm or cool, not to mention keep all your appliances running? Oh, why don't you try to eat Google or Facebook, we are very sure how nutritious they are. You don't know how to do all the things we know how to do easily. If you think you can farm by google, go ahead and try. We will enjoy watching you. But besides that, most of you are in your wonderful big cities. How long can you go without food? Heat? Because if you start a war, you're not getting fed for sure! It's frankly very easy to cut that off. Also remember, you call us *fly-over-country*. You think we'll let you fly over? Leave us alone and we'll provide you the goods and services at a fair price."

Of course, during the standoff, you build up your military defenses because you know the left is insane and self-destructive. But the point is, you actually do have the ability to halt the abuse you are suffering now and the *terrible* abuse they plan for you. You can forestall it for at least a generation and maybe more. But this becomes even more beautiful, because you know within your Red States you have pockets of blue. Well, if you had the power, and you can, what would you do with them, good Christians? How about I remind you of what I told the children of Israel when I described how they should set up their nation?

Do you really want Sodomites in your land? Drug addicts? *Drug pushers?* You could in fact shut it all down within your Red State borders if you really wanted to. And to all those in those wretched conditions you say, "Look. We can't have this amongst us anymore. You Sodomites. Pick a wonderful blue city like LA, San Fran, NYC, Chicago, of your choice and we will give you a one way ticket there, on our dime.... Ahhh, *don't come back!*"

WHAT CAN BE DONE TO DELAY THE BEAST?

To those dealing drugs, "Look. Forewarning. Those caught dealing drugs will be put to death. Period. You have one month to spread the word and then you *will* see it happen if you continue in such destruction." To the drug addicts and others who hate the natural consciousness of life I give them, you say, "Look. We are locking you up, drying you out, and training you if you need it, to be productive. Then we'll give you a good start in your life. Screw up again and we have a one way ticket out for you. *Don't come back."*

You see, conservative Christians be you Baptist, Methodist, Pentecostal etc., these is a lot you can agree on. And your schools, *public* schools will have no more offensive teaching within them. You see, all you folks, you actually *know* how to live, but you have let your *responsibility* to society and community be *completely* run over by Satan. You have let him neuter you, but unlike a steer, or capon, and such, who have worth upon the butcher block, you have societally become... *what?*

Let me assure you that you *do not* have that much time to accomplish, to set this all up, because the Beast is very aware of your potential. Also, it will take you some years to put this all together, but you can, if your love for my goodness that you all *claim* you have in common is strong enough. How can this all happen?

Come together you conservative so-called *pastors, leaders* of your flocks from all across the United States! I already have in place the talent, the wisdom and the means to perform all this *if* you can simply unite on the basics. Then all the right folks will come together to help perform it! You *already* have all the resources you will need *if* you cooperate together. But what if you *don't?* What if you continue in the very same good *rut* that you have been in for about two-thousand years, since the time you were poisoned, since the time my holy people were sadly no longer respected amongst you?

While I am sure about your faith in my name, that though you are stuck in the middle of Jacob's ladder and that you won't take a step down, but you can't seem to take a step up, that if anyone told you to deny Me or they would kill you, I am sure you would say to just kill you. But the Beast isn't going to make it anywhere near that easy. Affliction and tribulation as was not ever seen, no, not since the world began, nor ever shall be, shall be upon *you*, upon all your loved ones, children, friends, family... And it all shall be put into great affliction for a singular purpose. To break your faith, to turn you against the very Essence of Reality which is me. Behold, I have told you, and as you see that from cover to cover in this work of *fiction*, that it is only truth, this is a witness for you or against you. Your choice.

CHAPTER 15

IN CONCLUSION TO THE BITTER END

The prophet Daniel, and John the Revelator, but others, as well, got a glimpse of the end times like a fast forward film strip from their time, into the future and the final end. They wrote what they could but it's the Holy Ghost, and *only* the Holy Ghost that can navigate you through what you must endure. The *Bible* has no ability to do this for you. Only My Word, which *is* My Spirit, and for you, the Holy Ghost, is able to give you the love and understanding and strength you need. The circumstances through the world will be quite varied in corruption, and swirling like a flushing toilet! And that *flushing* will seem like an eternity, with all the mire swirling around you.

Hatred will claw at you. The wicked will increasingly sense your presence because the presence of righteousness, or holiness, will become more evident to them, but they won't see it as good. As it is written, some of you will be imprisoned, mocked, humiliated, tortured, and others will be killed quickly. Yet, others will have power to stand against them.

What I hate most is those of you who are overcome with fear. That fear is you bowing to your enemy, which they revel in. But they lack compassion, I want you to understand that. To them, you *deserve* the foul treatment they will heap on you and your fear just increases their pleasure. They are driven by Satan in his fury because you have the utter gall to hold to the name of Jesus, you pathetic, mere mortal balls of clay. But *that's* what *I* love so much about you!

And another irony? To Satan, those doing his evil bidding are fools, dumb beasts without a mind or sense, and no matter how far evil he twists them into, it doesn't satisfy Satan. He *does* get satisfaction from making the righteous and the holy to suffer, though. He feels they are insulting to him! These fleshly imposters of a *being*. And it's so *very* easy to afflict them.

Do you understand what you are up against? If you seek Me, I can prepare you to stand with integrity no matter what. But if you do, that will anger them even more! But there comes a point during this dark ritual of theirs, where, believe it or not, you will begin to enjoy it! What I mean is, you will see inside yourselves a steadfastness in goodness, a love for Goodness that just can't be dissuaded, corrupted, or even successfully challenged. And when you see *that* inside yourselves, you'll also see Peace! I know. I was there!

At that point, open your mouths and I will give you what to say! And *I* will give you what to do. But *between* then and now, what *can* you do? The purpose of this *fiction* is to shine light where none has shined, and by *that,* to open your hearts and minds to understand more, acquire more strength, and secure your faith. There are prayers for every single individual to pray, prayers *only* for each individual! Those are the prayers you need to find because they open the door

~ IN CONCLUSION TO THE BITTER END ~

to your soul, your heart, your mind where I can give each and every one of you what is specifically for you and you alone!

But dear Christians, what if the processes you have developed within your worship style would cut off the answer to the prayers I have for you? Have you noticed that even on many of your websites you have something akin to the following: We are a Bible believing church, we uphold the Word of God as written in . . . and some prefer Kings James, I know I do, but others feel more comfortable with a different translation. Nevertheless, you measure everything, and I mean *everything,* by the processes you have developed around the *written* word of God.

If anyone mentions something about Me, the first thing you ask is, Where is that in the Scriptures. Now, the other person might have communicated an exactly true *meaning* to you, but somehow, if it's not the *exact* words of the Holy Scripture, you don't trust it. But even more importantly, you do the *exact* same things to your own selves! If a thought, or a feeling comes to you, whether it's of My Goodness, or the goodness I made you out of, or a new goodness naturally extending from those, the first thing you do is try to find whether it matches My printed word. If you can't find the match, you throw it out.

Here is My question to you, dear Christians: Can My printed Word contain Me? Can it encompass My Spirit? Can it be the right emotion at the right time? Can it deepen your feelings within righteousness where you had not deepened before? Can it *be* those feelings? And if they are *new* feelings, how do you then trust them if you can't find them in the Scripture? Will those feelings even be around by the time you finish searching my printed word?

My Holy Scripture, inspired *directly* by Me, is like a cab you catch to travel to a destination. It can carry you to the door, but it *can't* drive through! Not only that, but you must pick yourselves up, get out of that basically metal box, walk up to the door, knock, and when it opens, you must walk in. The cab does not partake of all that *experience*. But you *Christians* like to travel *a lot* but you never get out of the cab.

Holy Scriptures are supposed to help you, in part, on your journey, but *I AM* supposed to be your *experience!* In other words, *I* bring you new thoughts, new feelings for you to grow by, for you to *be* by. I AM is a state of Holy Consciousness, omniscient, omnipresent, and to be *clear,* omni-experiencing all things! And just like I, the Lord Jesus Christ, gave up my omnipresence so that I could, for Myself for your sake, *experience* humanity and direct evil contact, *you* need to allow yourselves to *fully* experience Me, My Holy Presence as I bring it to you.

Dear Christians, experiencing My Presence is so far beyond any processes you conduct relating to my Holy Scripture that if you in any way try to match this up, it would be like trying to fit a whole rainstorm into a teacup.

There is a 'feel' to my Holy Presence, and within that general feeling an infinity opens to you and you will be attracted to a certain part of that infinity unique for you. How are you going to try and match your written word processes to that? If you try to, you cut the holy experience off because a holy *experience* has processes in you that engage far beyond anything you normally experience. If you allow yourselves to *experience* Me, you will be changed for the better and very new processes form in you. After that happens you will look at the Holy Scripture like people today would look at a manual typewriter which is powered not by electricity but only by many hard finger strikes.

That just spoken to you scares you, I know. But why? Please pay close consideration to this I explain to you. The world, Satan, plays a game with short-, medium-, and long-term strategies. The Holy Scriptures are fine for interdicting a lot of the first two but *not* the long term. The long term evolves from *states of consciousness!* Let Me explain.

The World has attacked you for millennia, and it has desecrated and attacked My written Word. Also, in the *Old* Testament there was much focus on the written Word with commands to write it down, speak of it often, and follow it. But it was the *meaning,* the *true meaning,* and *true love* I was after. Nevertheless, my command was to keep my Word, which was written even in stone for My chosen people. But *what* did they of old *use* to keep my Word? They used their own *will.* The *same* will that failed Adam and Eve. *That* will *cannot* contain or assimilate the *new* will, the *new* heart, the *new* spirit I made for you. *That's* why I require you to give *everything* back to Me! *Everything* is contained within your whole will!

Everything includes the processes you use to serve Me through My written Word! Because the new process for My new service originate within and go out from a *new* state of consciousness that I will give you when you are truly born again by receiving my Holy Ghost! All this I speak to you is actually foretold to you in My written Word!

Are you Christians feeling very uncomfortable with this? Why? Not only from what I mentioned to you about the Old Testament, but as I said to you, the World has attacked you for millennia, and it has desecrated and attacked My written Word in *many* ways. *Many* religions have sprung up around My name so which one is right, which one is true? And which translation? And *then* you have those *geniuses* I have taken *particular* time to describe to you. It is *they* who have speared you through the heart with the long-term destructive strategies I mentioned earlier.

They vehemently assault your faith *and* your knowledge of Me. *That* assault tends to drive you to the Holy Scriptures and to hold on to them with tenacity. And then they pound you with, *How do you* know *they are from God.* Men wrote . . . bla, bla, bla! All of *that* causes you to triple down on your focus of the written word and *lock you* into those *OLD* processes!

And *then,* you make a statement to *protect* you and your loved ones, you say all knowledge of Me comes from My written Word. *Please* think about this: How did you first *know* I AM the only begotten Son of the Living God? Was it just from reading it? Many have read and not believed. Some believed for a time and then turned away. Was it because you heard Me preached to you? Again, many have heard that sound and not believed and some have believed for a time then renegued.

What's your answer? How did you first *know* I AM the only begotten Son of the Living God? Faith? How? Please, look inside yourselves and see the *how* that you *don't merely believe* in Me, but you *know* I AM REAL! You know it, you feel it down to your marrow in your spiritual bones. But how?

Because, from the goodness I made you out of, your little goodness *recognizes* My Goodness from whence you came. The knowledge of Being is real in your souls and recognizes in a very fundamental way that My BEING, My Essence of Reality eternally encompasses yours! *And* you *know* that is Goodness, and you *know* what Goodness will Be, will do, *how* Goodness will Love! And *that,* My dear friends, is *how you know* I AM the only begotten Son of the Living God.

And not only that. Yes, there's even more in you than you *verbally* realize! You also *know* that I AM the greatest, the utmost of all goodness! Think about that. Not *just* that I am perfect, but that there are no other perfections that even come close to rivaling Me! And not

~ IN CONCLUSION TO THE BITTER END ~

only *that!* You *know* this from even the *tiniest* experience you have with My Spirit! Why? Because My innate quality permeates Me through even the *tiniest* of all that I AM and *you*, yes, YOU recognize this and *know* it. *All that* is from where your faith comes! Am I speaking the truth? Think about it. Think about it like you have never thought before, like your very lives depend on it, because they do!

You see why I still love you in *spite* of your shortcomings I described earlier? You see why I am pleading with you? And now you are ready to hear: Your faith did not, *could not* come from My Holy Scriptures! Nor any preaching. Your faith came from the recognition you have of Me as I just described. Hearing My Word just initially helps put perspective to it. But the long-term *trick* that Satan has pulled on you by focusing you solely on My printed word has actually driven you *away* from your faith! Away from your internal processes that produce that treasured faith! That *trick* locks you out of receiving My new heart and new spirit I made for you, or, if you managed to receive it, that *trick* keeps you from accessing the newness you have to its fullest potential!

In the same fashion as you have your true faith in Me, you need, through the knowledge of that faith, a knowledge which is *not* merely a mental knowing, but mind and heart into one. It's love, and life, and justice, and peace, and truth, and wisdom, and understanding in you all in One. You need to come fully to Me and *experience* My fullness that I have for you, and *not* just experience it, you need to allow me to have *full* control of you, meaning, give Me your whole will, give it fully back to Me, so I can come fully into you and give you a new one!

Let Me in. *Experience* Me within you. I will not destroy the goodness you give Me. I will make it stronger, better, with the glory My Father has given Me to give you! I love you. Now, let us go hence?

www.ingramcontent.com/pod-product-compliance
Lightning Source LLC
Chambersburg PA
CBHW070352120526
44590CB00014B/1109